WTO and Its Implication to Higher Education in India

Opportunities and Challenges

Malleshi, N. Siddalingappanavar

CONCEPT PUBLISHING COMPANY PVT. LTD.
NEW DELHI-110059

ISBN-13: 978-93-5125-009-8

First Published 2014

Published and Printed by

Since 1974

Concept Publishing Company Pvt. Ltd.
A/15-16, Commercial Block, Mohan Garden
New Delhi-110059 (India)
T: 25351460, 25351794, *F*: 091-11-25357109
E: publishing@conceptpub.com, W: www.conceptpub.com
Editorial Office: H-13, Bali Nagar, New Delhi-110 015, India.

Cataloging in Publication Data--Courtesy: D.K. Agencies (P) Ltd. <docinfo@dkagencies.com>

Siddalingappanavar, Malleshi N.
WTO and its implication to higher education in India : opportunities and challenges/ Malleshi N. Siddalingappanavar.
p. cm.
Originally presented as the author's thesis (Ph. D.).
Includes bibliographical references (p.) and index.
ISBN 9789351250098

1. Higher education and state—India. 2. World Trade Organization—India. 3. General Agreement on Trade in Services (1994). I. Title. II. Title: World Trade Organization and its implication to higher education in India.

DDC 378.54 23

Foreword

There is a new understanding of Nationhood; there is a new pace set by the compulsions of time targets defined by global initiations like the World Trade Organization. In a bid to register higher rates of economic growth, there is a new challenge for the policy makers to accelerate flow of international capital, technology and trade, yet preserve the independence of our institutions, and strengthen our pride in them. Each segment of the Indian economy must find a new zeal to rapidly gain international competitiveness, the new "Mantra," the effective practice of which will determine the economic well-being of the nation.

Dr. Siddalingappanavar's analytical work on WTO and its Implication to Higher Education in India provides useful guidance to stakeholders and policy makers of education to prepare the eventuality of WTO agreements. The statistical data and the evidence, implications of articles put forth in this study, Dr. Siddalingappanavar hopes, "helps stakeholders of higher education and policy makers in deciding the type of policy intervention needed to tackle the issues of WTO agreements, entry of foreign institutions/universities, of student mobility and host of other things in India". In this sense, Dr. Siddalingappanvar's study is an important contribution to the corpus of implication literature on the subject.

The analysis of GATS article-wise and mode-wise implications of WTO on higher education services in the context of India is presented in the book, no doubt, yields valuable insights into the role of WTO agreements for modification of higher education system. The book intensively analyzes the student mobility under pre- and post-WTO periods; which assist to derive specific policy inputs. The subject matter had acquired a contemporary relevance in the current discussion on internationalization of higher education.

In the sixty-first year of the Republic of India, Parliament has enacted the Foreign Educational Institutions (Regulation of Entry and Operations) Act, 2010; which lead to entry of foreign universities in India may provide huge opportunities and challenges to higher education system, it stimulated the stakeholders of education to rethink their ways of working and improve the quality of higher education. In this connection, the book suggests certain important measures to inculcate in the system of higher education.

From all points of view, this book provides a new insight into GATS implications to trade in higher education services; since higher education is playing a catalytic role in the rapid development of the country. This will not only continue to assist the policy makers but also inspire researcher to take up several issues of higher education under WTO agreements.

Further, intensive research work has to be done on the issues viz. Cross Border Supply Mode and Movement of Natural Persons Mode of trade in education services respectively. Under the Movement of Natural Persons mode India has competitive advantage over developed countries of the world; India ought to reap the demographic dividend of the country in this respect. I do hope that Dr. Siddalingappanvar will carry forward his study to tackle these issues so that he can provide concrete policy inputs.

H.H. Uliveppa
07 June, 2012 Professor of Economics
Department of Studies and Research in Economics
Karnataka University
Dharward

Preface

The role of higher education in the development of the economy, science and technology as well as other spheres of life has been well recognized. The institutions of higher education have been able to provide a strong base of an educated workforce in the areas of agriculture, technology, medicine, social sciences, general sciences, arts and literature.

The Higher education service comes under the WTO's GATS agreement; as right now, very limited studies are concentrated on the issue of higher education in the context of GATS; in this connection, the present study is a unique of its kind; it contributes to the enrichment of literature in the field of higher education with reference to GATS.

The book is organized into seven chapters. Chapter 1 presents the research design, covering significance of the study, research issues and database and limitations. Chapter 2 provides an issue-wise thorough review of literature on internationalization of higher education and identifies a wide range of issues for research. A brief historical perspective of higher education in India is provided in Chapter 3. An Overview of the World Trade Organization (WTO), General Agreement on Trade in Services (GATS) and summary of the commitment made by WTO's member nations on education sector is presented in Chapter 4. An analysis relating to the GATS article-wise implications on Indian higher education is provided in Chapter 5 Chapter 6, the mode-wise analysis of trade in higher education services and the data on trends of Foreign Students Inflow and Indian Students Outflow by year-wise, sex-wise, subject-wise, country-wise, continent-wise, source of financial assistance for outflow are analyzed in detail, further opportunities and challenges of higher education services are evaluated. The last Chapter contains a summary of findings and important policy recommendations.

This book will be useful to researchers, stakeholders and policy makers in deciding the type of policy intervention needed to tackle the problems of higher education under WTO regime.

Bagalkot
June 2012

M.N. Siddalingappanavar

Acknowledgements

Pursuance of research on issues relating the developments and changes of higher education, impact of globalization and WTO agreement, trends in student mobility for higher studies the research inputs being obtained from many academicians and also unstinted support from many well-wishers. During the course of my research work, I have received continuous advice, guidance and assistance from my research guide, academicians and friends, for which it is my great privilege to acknowledge their contributions.

I express my profound sense of gratitude to my research guide Dr. H. H. Uliveppa, Professor in Economics, Department of Studies and Research in Economics, Karnataka University, Dharwad, who inspired, fostered and channelised my efforts. I owe him a lot for his excellent guidance, constant encouragement; which enabled me to do the best of my ability in completing my research work.

I sincerely express thankfulness to Prof. H. B. Walikar, Vice Chancellor, Karnataka University, Dharwad for his advice and blessings. I place on record my sense of gratitude to my teachers, Prof. S.T. Bagalkoti, Prof. L. D. Vaikunthe, Dr. R. R. Biradar for their critical comments and suggestions on an earlier version of the book. I am thankful to Prof. P. M. Honakeri, Dr. Talwar Sabanna, Dr. D. N. Patil for their valuable suggestion during the course of my research work.

I express my gratitude and heartfelt thanks to Dr. H. G. Jambagi, Sri. S. U. Ganachri, Dr. Sanjeev Kenchaigoal, Dr. Hanumagouda Patil, Dr. Myageri, Dr. Uttam Kamble, Dr. Vijay Laxmi Hegade, Dr. Saraswati Bommanal, Dr. Pallavi Kusugal for their friendly help and support during my doctoral work.

I am very much thankful to National Social Science Documentation Centre (NASSDOC), Indian Council of Social Science Research (ICSSR), New Delhi for its financial assistance under Study Grants Scheme for my research work.

In pursuance of my research work for Ph.D. degree, I have been greatly benefited from several libraries at Karnataka University, Dharwad, Centre for Multi-disciplinary Research, Dharwad, Institute for Social and Economic Change (ISEC), Bangalore, Jawaharlal Nehru University (JNU), New Delhi, National Social Science Documentation Centre (NASSDOC), ICSSR, New Delhi, National Institute of Educational Planning and Administration (NIEPA), New Delhi, Association of Indian Universities (AIU), New Delhi, Indian Council for Research on International Economic Relations (ICRIER), New Delhi. Therefore, I am thankful to the officials of all libraries, who extended their kind co-operation in collection of data and literature. I am deeply indebted to my parents, wife, daughter, brother, sister and elder people for their co-operation in completion of the work. It is needless to mention that the author alone should be held responsible for any shortcomings.

I dedicate this work to my parents and teachers with all due reverence.

Malleshi, N. Siddalingappanavar

Contents

List of Tables

List of Figures

List of Charts

1

Research Issues and Approach

Introduction

In the developments which have taken place in various countries, besides their endowment of natural resources, the quality of their human resources have also played a critical role and it is important to note in this context that the quality of human resources is dependent on the level of knowledge, skills and the attitudes/values prevailing among the people. These, in turn, are determined by the achievement of the levels of schooling and higher education among the people. In the development of knowledge, higher education is pivotal and could be said to be the number of the professions. In the new era of liberalization and globalization, knowledge has assumed the form of intellectual property. Only those countries with a high quality of higher education can emerge as rich repositories of knowledge and get the full benefit of the new World Trade Organisation (WTO) agreement. These new agreements have brought sea change in all activities and sectors of the economy; the earlier barriers and restrictions on trade, movement of persons, capital, goods and services are relieved. Further, the agreements of WTO and General Agreement on Trade in Services (GATS) have fueled the process of liberalization and significantly the structure of higher education system is changing. The heydays of traditional Universities, with their campuses, lecture-rooms and flesh-and-bone teachers are perhaps going to be over (Dhar and Dhar, 2001). At the same time, the quality and competence have become prerequisite factors for survival of individuals, industries, products and services; these aspects can be acquainted through the system of education in general and higher education in particular; in this connection, education institutions must have the quality and market value in their products (courses); because students are become supreme agents in determining the fate of education institutions. As Nuna Sheela (2004) observed that Consumers of education today have profound influence on education system. They in a way dictate what education ought to be and look forward toward providers who satisfy their aspirations. Therefore, the existing higher education system has to review its structure through adopting need based international level curricula, quality, infrastructure, competence and relevance; otherwise the pressure on higher education is bound to increase in future. It is, therefore, high time that the universities and higher education system gears itself to face the demands and challenges of globalization.

The Higher Education is faced with newer challenges emerging out of an unprecedented changes taking place in different areas of the global plane. Expansions of knowledge and information technology have added new dimensions to this area. In view of this, higher education in the country needs to be transformed, supported and empowered accordingly. While quality and relevance of our higher education is a big concern, the lack of access and equity in higher education is no less important. In fact, promoting research and development, modern management in education, promoting basic sciences, education under GATS, etc. are the areas, which require immediate attention and these could be achieved only after the nation has a world-class university and higher education system. On the other hand, the education has been included as service under GATS; therefore the entry and growth of private initiatives in higher education sector is taking place and this trend is going to get further momentum in future. Hence, at this juncture the study on WTO and higher education is need of the hour; it contributes required information to policy makers in the said field.

Relevance of Higher Education

The higher education service comes under the WTO's GATS agreement; since India is founder member of WTO and its all general agreements apply to its member nations, but with specific agreement, nations will made commitment for them. Hence, there is an urgent need to focus on the GATS implications on higher education service to face the future eventuality successfully and to get maximum benefits from WTO agreements. Moreover, very limited studies are concentrated on the issue of higher education in the context of GATS; in this connection, the present study is a unique of its kind; it contributes to the enrichment of literature in the field of higher education with reference to GATS.

The importance of education services in promoting economic development is increasing. The higher education services are on the rise at international level and it is a potential area for trade; many developed countries are generating good revenue from trade in education. In this connection, it is peak time for India to chalk out a suitable strategy for its higher education system. The present study is an implication study; it makes useful contribution to the knowledge of higher education in the context of WTO regarding India's commitment to higher education under GATS agreements. The GATS article-wise, mode-wise trade in education services analysis and implications would be of immense help to the concerned agencies, research scholars and policy makers to take appropriate steps in future.

Research Issues

As is evident from the review of literature (*see* Chapter 2), little attention is paid to explore a satisfactory explanation of various aspects of development of higher education system since 1950. The extent of higher education development by growth of colleges and universities, sex-wise students enrolment, available teaching faculty, type of universities, discipline-wise distribution of students, subject-wise doctoral degrees, educational expenditure for different levels over a period have scarcely been studied under one roof. Hence, examining the development of higher education system at various aspects is also another area of research; further exploring the problems of higher education system in India is also quite essential for policy intervention under new economic policy and WTO's agreements. Moreover, there are few studies attempting to explore the implications of GATS articles on Indian higher education system.

Issues relating to the mode-wise[1] implications of trade in higher education services[2] of India have received little scholarly attention. An analysis of various aspects of Mode II is and causes of student mobility are required to be attempted. The analysis of these issues would certainly help stakeholders of higher education and policy makers in deciding the type of policy intervention needed to tackle the issues of WTO agreements, entry of foreign institutions/ universities, of student mobility and host of other things in India.

Against this background, the author has attempted to review the studies relating to different aspects of globalisation and internationalisation of higher education[3] in India; examine the development of higher education over ancient period, medieval period, under British rule and post-independence period; glancing an overview of the WTO's General Agreement on Trade in Services and summary of the commitment made by WTO's member nations on education sector is presented; analyze the GATS article-wise implications on Indian higher education; intensively analyze mode-wise implications of trade in higher education services in general and particularly the Consumption Abroad mode data on trends of Foreign Students Inflow and Indian Students Outflow by year-wise, sex-wise, subject-wise, country-wise, continent-wise, source of financial assistance for outflow; further evaluate opportunities and challenges of higher education services; and offer policy prescriptions for India's higher education services.

Database and Limitations

Nature and Coverage of Data

The present study is an implication study; which is a diagnostic one; two dimensional implications are considered in the study. On the one hand, the GATS's article-wise analysis and implications to Indian higher education system; on the other hand, mode-wise implications and analysis of trade in higher education services have been drawn; however limitation in access to data only mode II, i.e. Consumption Abroad related data is collected and analyzed exhaustively.

The study is based on secondary data collected from the various reports on the different aspects of foreign students' inflow and Indian students outflow by the Ministry of Human Resource Development (MHRD) of the Indian Students/Trainees Going Abroad, the Selected Educational Statistics and other documents. These reports/documents are the only source for comprehensive, detailed and also more comparable data on continent-wise, nation-wise and state-wise student mobility figures. The MHRD has published the Indian Students/ Trainees Going Abroad reports/documents till 1998 and further data has been collected from various government reports/documents. Hence, the reference period of the present study chosen is from 1986-87 to 2001-02; later on the entire period has been classified into two periods, i.e. pre-WTO period (1986-87 to 1994-95) and post-WTO period (1995-96 to 2001-02). The trends related to foreign students' inflow and Indian students' outflow, i.e. year-wise, sex-wise, subject-wise, financial assistance-wise, field of study-wise, state-wise, country-wise and continent-wise have been analyzed; however the data on foreign students' inflow is collected till 2004-05. In view of limited access to the data on the level of international trade in higher education-related services on Indian context; the study limits itself for making WTO's GATS article-wise implication on Indian higher education and analyzing mode-wise implication of trade in higher education services. Further, only the data related to mode II i.e. consumption abroad is collected and analyzed; it has not touched the issues (agreements) viz. Trade Related Intellectual Property Rights (TRIPS) and Trade Related Investment Measures (TRIMS) and their implications to higher education.

The time series data on status of Indian higher education, i.e. growth of colleges and universities, growth of students enrolment and teachers, growth of type of institutions, sex-wise colleges and enrolment, discipline-wise doctoral degree awarded, educational expenditure as percentage of public expenditure and Gross Domestic Product (GDP) and different levels of educational expenditure under five year plans has been collected by various reports of University Grants Commission (UGC), MHRD and five year plans.

Further, the study utilises secondary information of publication and reports of World Trade Organization (WTO), World Bank, United Nations Educational Scientific and Cultural Organization (UNESCO), Department of Education, Planning, Monitoring and Statistics Division, Planning Commission, Association of Indian Universities and obtained from relevant published books, research papers, articles etc.

Tools of Data Analysis

In the present study, to analyze the trends of student mobility (foreign students' inflow and Indian students' outflow) across continent, country, state and subject tools like percentages and compound annual growth rates (CGR) have been used. To identify the status of higher education simple statistical tools viz. averages, percentages have been used.

Organization of the Book

The book is organized into 7 Chapters. Chapter 1 presents the introduction and research methodology covering significance of the study, research issues, objectives, database and limitations. Chapter 2 comprehensively put forward review of literature on globalisation of higher education and identifies a wide range of issues for research. A brief historical perspective of higher education in India, focusing on the education system in Ancient India, Medieval Period, during British rule and Post-Independence period—specifically growth and present status is provided in Chapter 3. An Overview of the World Trade Organisation (WTO), General Agreement on Trade in Services (GATS) and summary of the commitment made by WTO's member nations on education sector is presented in Chapter 4. An analysis relating to the GATS article-wise implications on Indian higher education is provided in Chapter 5. In Chapter 6, the mode-wise analysis viz. Cross Border Supply, Consumption Abroad, Commercial Presence and Presence of Natural Persons of trade in higher education services and the data on trends of Foreign Students' Inflow and Indian Students' Outflow by year-wise, sex-wise, subject-wise, country-wise, continent-wise, source of financial assistance for outflow are analyzed in detail, further opportunities and challenges of higher education services are evaluated. The last Chapter contains a summary of findings and important policy recommendations.

Notes

1. Education services are traded through four modes under WTO viz. Cross Border Supply, Consumption Abroad, Commercial Presence and Presence of Natural Person. In course of analysis and discussion; the terms Cross Border Supply, Consumption Abroad, Commercial Presence and Presence of Natural Person are used interchangeably to Mode I, Mode II, Mode III and Mode IV respectively.
2. The act of exchanging commodities/services for money; it is nothing but business of buying and selling. Here, universities/colleges, students/parents, institutions/countries, teachers/researchers/skilled and semi-skilled education service providers are important stakeholders. Education services can be traded through four modes.

3. There is a difference between globalisation and Internationalisation of higher education; Globalisation of Higher education refers to "the trends in higher education that have cross-national implications, including mass higher education and a global marketplace for students, faculty and highly educated personnel as well as the global reach of the new Internet-based technologies". Internationalisation of higher education is the specific policies and initiative of countries and individual academic institutions or systems to deal with global trends (Altbach, 2002).

2

World Trade Organisation and Its Implication to Higher Education in India

A Review of Literature and Issues for Research

Introduction

There are very limited studies made by Indian scholars to evaluate the Indian higher education system under WTO's GATS context; among them few studies are appeared on issues viz. globalization and internationalization of higher education, functioning of foreign education institutions. However an intensive mode-wise analysis of higher education services is need of the hour under WTO regime. Hence, there is a need for making the detailed review of literature on the present study to know the existing status of the problem, so that the researcher would be able to make an improvement over the existing studies and also expand the horizon of investigation on the subject matter. In this chapter, an attempt has been made to review the important studies on development of higher education, implications of GATS agreements and of mode-wise trade in higher education services, trends of student mobility and identify research gaps for the present study.

Higher Education Issues and Quality

A study by Trivedi (2010) examined the dilemma of giving commercial treatment to Indian higher education and it discusses several aspects to improve the quality of higher education. Firstly, the academic audit is required more for enhancing the quality; secondly, the various stages[1] based and quality based education must be provided at each stage. The leakage of any stage would disturb the quality of the next stage and the whole purpose of education could not be served. Further, the study analyzed the role of government, regulatory bodies, teachers and students in enhancing the quality of higher education.

A study by Akhtar (2012) has analyzed the importance of academic quality and reasons for poor quality of higher education. Academic quality provides learning opportunities for students, which help them to achieve their award. Academic quality is about making sure that appropriate and effective teaching, support, assessment and learning opportunities are provided. The problem of poor quality just surfaces out at higher education stage. Actually, the problem lies at the grass root level where the students getting sub-standard primary and secondary education join the higher education. Finally, the study brought out certain remedies that the quality in higher education can be improved by developing and using well accepted learning resources, encouraging teachers to learn tools and methodologies, using sound evaluation schemes, continuous feedback evaluation and providing rich and healthy environment.

A study by Gupta (2011) examined the current status of higher education in the country; there has been a substantial increase in the number of educational institutions in recent years; where the quality of education provided has been an area of concern. The study found that, according to industry estimates, only a quarter of all graduates are employable and 80 per cent of the job seekers in employment exchanges are without any professional skills. There is a huge gap on the specialized skill front and the question is how to get highly qualified and skilled people. The study observed following suggestions. Firstly, linkage between school education and higher education should be strengthened; secondly, the government should subsidise individuals instead of institutions through easy loans, scholarships; thirdly, the government is required to be spent at least 1.5 per cent of GDP as against 0.7 per cent on higher education. Finally, the mechanisms should be developed to attract leading Indian faculty from universities of abroad.

Financing of Higher Education

A study by Hussain (2000) highlighted various challenges in the field of higher education and ascertains time-bound action plans to solve them. Increasing population and increasing financial burden on the conventional education has become a big challenge, where distance education can cater the increasing demand for education problem through educating the masses. Similar observation made by Sethi Priyanka and Saharan (2010) that open universities need to be encouraged to offer quality programmes at the least cost; this becomes the most cost-effective way of providing higher education, including technical and vocational education.

For solving the problem of finance privatization of education may be a necessary step; for this a proper planning for incorporating the idea of privatization is recommended. Further, the study suggested the establishment of Self-financing units, imparting vocational and technical education. A similar observation is made by Prasad (2001) that higher education institutions are necessary to augment cost recoveries from students through tuition fees and other charges and need to introduce comprehensive scheme of loan assistance so as to, eventually, develop a self-generating and self-sustaining fund; further autonomy to colleges/institutions, continuation of government support to higher education institutions is needed.

A study by Sethi Priyanka and Saharan (2010) suggested that, the need for financing of higher education for students, especially those coming from low income households needs special attention; subsidization of interest rate for students should be based on his family income. For this innovative financial mechanism needs to be evolved incorporating some of the salient features of the systems existing in UK and USA. Further it was observed that, the issue of raising the fees upwards to meet the cost of education is critical if we are to maintain and sustain the quality of our government and aided private institutions are already using a higher fee structure.

A study by Srinivas (2011) observed the role of Central and State Governments, self-financing system, grant-in-aid system, public-private partnership, foreign educational institutions and fee reimbursement system of financing of higher education. The study more intensively discussed the suggestions for financing of higher education during Twelfth Five Year Plan. The critical issue is that none of the statutory or funding agencies could be able to address the declining role of government in non-recruitment of teachers for decades together and ban on creation of new teaching, non-teaching positions in higher education. The study suggested, firstly differential treatment to universities, national institutions and colleges in financial assistance or incentives should end. Secondly, norms based funding is being thought out as a best method; any amount of financial assistance will go waste without addressing these issues. Further, non-lapsable funding system is needed for higher education institutions.

New Economic Policy[2] and Higher Education

A study by Altbach (2000) discussed the working of multinational higher education institutions. The motive for establishing multinational higher education enterprises is almost always to make money. The multinational and distance movement does not really contribute to the internationalization of higher education[3] worldwide; because there is little mutual exchange of ideas, long-term scientific collaboration, exchange of students or faculty. The study listed few facts on new multinational and distance phenomena. It operates in a largely unregulated environment and as the economists stated it as "demand absorbing". They provide access at a very low price to those who seek it. Finally, the study pointed out that multinational higher education is a big business, and it is about to get much bigger. For example the Jones International University and America's private institute i.e. The University of Phoenix not really universities although they have the term in their titles. They do not have regular faculty, nor is there any kind of participatory governance system typical of universities rather, they are degree delivery machines.

A study by Biswas (2001) has examined the ethics of globalization and its impact on education; it observed that international partnership arrangements are guided by profits than services. The cumulative effect of the operational dynamics of WTO as a global force has fractured the very purpose of education in India. In an attempt to arrive at a cultural homogeneity, it is arriving at cultural fragmentation. Further, study pointed out that higher education in India may be gaining relevance and prominence in global platform; but as a cost of success is compromising on its relevance for the Indian setting.

A study by Prasad (2001) suggested several measures needed to adopt underglobalization of higher education.[4] (1) the universities to equip themselves with the knowledge tools and administrative flexibilities to meet the competition globally; (2) the universities may have to develop an attitude by which students will be treated as clients with continuously changing needs and ambitions, the curriculum would require constant change; (3) globalization of higher education will require definitive changes including the strengthening of infrastructure, creation of additional seats, streamlining of admission procedures, version of curricula to include global component. Further, the study strongly supported the promotion of globalization of higher education not only because of financial benefits but also because of the academic, political and social advantages that accrue from the presence of international students on campuses.

A study by Sharma and Maheshwari (2004) discussed the internationalization of higher education situation in India; it found that India is attracting less number of foreign students from developed countries, but it is attracting relatively high number of students from developing countries like Kenya, Nepal, Bangladesh, Srilanka, etc. Finally, study suggested several factors for internationalization of higher education and trade in education service has to be more on business line with minimum government controls. Private participation has to be accredited by internationally so as to ensure international quality.

A study by Agarwal (2006) has analyzed the advantages of liberalization of higher education; the policy promotes the quality of domestic education system, attracting foreign students and research will fuel innovation and enterprise in the higher education system. The study suggested the measures to maximize its benefits in higher education system: (1) people should have realistic expectations as regards public policy towards higher education sector; (2) implementing the public policy of maintaining standards of Indian higher education at benchmark with the global standards, which gives the India a distinctive competitive edge in global labour markets; (3) for global recognition of its qualifications, India needs to work towards the harmonization of its academic standards with internationally accepted practices; (4) it should follow investment-friendly and forward-looking domestic regulation; (5) the loopholes in the existing system need to be plugged to enhance the credibility of an academic qualification from India; (6) finally, an effective system of registration has to be put in place to prevent unapproved foreign institutions from operating in India and to ensure that students are not exploited.

A study by Uliveppa and Siddalingappanavar (2006) examined the issue of internationalization of higher education by applying SWOT (Strengths, Weakness, Opportunities and Threats) analysis. The study observed the India's great strength in several aspects for creating much conducive environment for internationalization viz. having large and powerful higher educational set up, English as medium of instruction, large pool of variety of skilled human resource, economics of fees and living expenses and India's lead in ICT sector. On the other hand, it found dangers from internationalization viz. possibility of commercialization of higher education, take-over of universities/colleges by the foreign corporate houses, public higher education may lose its existence, concentration of institutions on urban areas and brain drain.

Finally, the study suggested some measure for harnessing the opportunities of internationalization of higher education: (1) Indian Embassies and High Commissions should take initiative in providing information about its higher education system; (2) simplification of visa issuing and extension policy; (3) establishment of agency for maintaining database; (4) setting up of mechanism for monitoring the standard of foreign universities and Indian universities/institutions to improve their academic and infrastructural quality; further internationalization of curricula is needed.

A study by Raghavan (2011) has assessed the impact of LPG policy on education sector; it argues that opening up of education sector for private universities would lead to competition, which may boost up economic growth whereas competition devalues quality of education. Similarly, the crisis in university education is mainly a crisis of liberal education and now a days; universities are not concerned with moral and intellectual health of the society. The study recommended that: (1) the university curriculum has to be made more inclusive in the sense that it is integrative to multiple domains looking at them from their distinct perspectives; (2) teachers must direct the students for realizing their passion, ideals and potential. (3) government must run universities towards quality, innovation and high order thinking in our students; because the private universities are only concerned towards profit and little bother about the earlier aspects. Finally, in order to face the LPG policy very effectively, the government should spend the money on improving existing colleges and setting up new ones to offer students education for life and citizenship.

GATS Implication on Higher Education

A study by Sahni and Kale (2004) has discussed the present system of higher education and attempted to find the possible implications for India in being a signatory to GATS. The study analyzed the broad structure of GATS and concentrated on some of its articles. It pointed out that the GATS agreements are in diverse; there are intrinsic pressures for pushing negotiations of 'interest groups'. In the absence of a coherent education policy, the effects of opening up could lead to a distorted function of education in Indian society. The Article of Transparency is an uneasy one especially for Third World countries, because it involves actually making the regulatory mechanism public. India faces many challenges in the regulatory mechanisms in higher education and the study highlighted that, opening up of the sector to international institutions could deep the regional disparity, at the same time foreign provider may only concentrate on management education, where they get maximum profit.

A study by Meena (2005) has observed that GATS is still an untested agreement on issues like Dispute Mechanism, Subsidies to education sector, Treatment of monopolies, Qualification requirements and procedures. Further, some concerns are articulated by the study e.g. domestic/national policies on education at risk, only those skills will be enhanced which have the potential of marketability, increase in costs and tuition fees; commercialization of education, indigenous and regional educational system overlooked, humanities and non-profitable subjects will suffer, problem of assessment and accreditation by different nations.

A study by Bolashetty (2005) has analyzed exclusively the article-wise implications of GATS on Indian education; and suggested for 'Impact Assessment Research Studies' on LPG process and stated that a thorough debate on the impact of GATS on education sector needed in the Parliament, State Legislatures and Academic Forums in India to base the LPG process on ethics and in the interest/common cause of every Indian citizen. The study suggested following measures: (1) Government of India should constitute an "Expert Commission" involving University Grants Commission, AIU, AICTE, NCTE, MCI, PCI, DCI, BCI, ICHR, ICPR, CSIR, NIEPS, NCERT, etc. The Commission should work on the issues viz. the reviewing of the experiences of GATS implementation in the developed countries, the implications of GATS on Indian Service Sectors with special emphasis on Education Sector in general and sub-sectors of Education in particular; (2) UGC and other autonomous central agencies of education should thoroughly study the 'strategies' employed by the developed countries to gain optimum benefits out of GATS; (3) each educational institution in India should prepare a 'strategic plan' to compete with its counterparts in other member countries of WTO; (4) the Universities should publish literature on GATS-literacy for creating Knowledge, Awareness and Practices (KAP) among all the concerned persons/individuals; (5) the Universities may establish WTO chairs to study the international legal agreements/instruments being worked out by WTO *vis-à-vis* India; (6) Government of India should establish an 'Expert Task Force' to assess, and accredit the quality and standards of service suppliers in India; (7) Government of India should provide enough funds to Indian service suppliers to raise themselves to the status of World Class based on highest international standards.

A study by Khajapeer (2004) has examined theoretical implications of GATS on Indian higher education system and analyzed the advantages and disadvantages of GATS entrance. Internationalization of higher education helps the indigenous education system to impart an international dimension into the learning, research and service functions. The quality of higher education might get a good boost in the country due to the demonstration effect of the foreign providers; further it increases the access to higher education and the investment in the infrastructure of higher education. It is necessary for India to resort its distance mode to achieve tangible result and to increase the enrolments in higher education. On the other hand, negative effects are highlighted viz. the possibility of emerging of two types of higher education system in the country, foreign provider may not serve the objective of the National Education Policy and there profit motives would prove to be disastrous, the threat of foreign dominance or exploitation of a national system and culture are the matter of serious concern.

A study by Sahni and Kale (2004) has analyzed GATS mode-wise implications of higher education services. Developed countries can get maximum benefit under Cross-border Supply Mode; whereas both developed and developing countries are competing with each other in Consumption Abroad Mode. U.S. has been leading one in attracting overseas students; for example, India and other countries in Southeast Asia have been attracting overseas students and which is improving. Developed nations are much interested in Commercial Presence Mode, because there is huge demand for higher education in developing countries like India and China, where foreigner can open their institutions and branches. It has been pointed out that if Indian Government committed for Commercial Presence Mode it may lead to 'domestic brain drain' (internal) of academicians within the field. In case of Presence of Natural Persons Mode developing countries have advantage over other countries; particularly India has a comparative advantage of utilizing its unused huge skilled and semi-skilled human resources. But developed countries are linking the Commercial Presence Mode with Presence of Natural Persons Mode; they are following tight immigration policy and issue of the recognition of qualifications of this Third World professional.

A study by Meena (2005) has focused on the base of India's responding to GATS issue, it discussed the issue in four segments, i.e. existing situation of higher education institutions in India, positive indicators for India to respond to GATS, drawbacks where efforts from India is needed and concerns over GATS. The study has apprehended that in future mode III and mode IV will be in stronger position in the global market for education services and mode I also grow at larger extent; at the same time mode II become smaller. Further, the study pointed out certain suggestions: (1) to take more advantage from GATS, there is a need to increase the number of technical and professional world standard institutions which can compete with other private and Foreign Service Providers; (2) India holds mastery compared to other nations in certain fields; because it can provide cost-effective education to foreign nations. Hence, the following areas must be explored viz. Yoga, Music, Fine Arts, Sanskrit language, Ayurveda, Homoeopathy, Unani, Naturotherapy, Computer Application, Computer Science by using the modes of e-learning, distance education, CDs and various audio-visual aids; (3) redefining the aims and objectives of higher education in GATS regime must be carried out and to be informed to the general public; (4) the whole functioning of the educational system needs transformation via organizational approach, revision of University acts, continuously updating of syllabi, working conditions, financial funding, academic staff, educational infrastructure, its administration, accreditation, assessment etc.

Cross Border Supply Mode

A study by Sukumar (2005) discussed the opportunities, the challenges and the desirable response to globalization of distance education; the following opportunities has been identified: (1) major policy reforms must be implemented, i.e. of structuring, funding and regulating the Indian Open Distance Learning (ODL) system and instead of too many regulators of ODL single regulatory body must be framed to solve the problems of ODL; (2) require closer links with Indian industry, especially the growing technology based sector and reputed higher learning institutions. Besides, it needs a globally oriented, entrepreneurial style of leadership and other top-level administrations; (3) the instant connectivity of resource persons and the easy accessibility of resource materials in distance education made possible by the communication, technologies, help in learning from others expertise and experience; (4) the educational needs of India can be met effectively by the collaboration arrangements particularly in the development of curriculum, which is a very capital-intensive activity in distance education. On the other hand, the study identified following challenges: (1) more access may result in the danger of certain sets of countries dominating the educational scene of countries with less resource; (2) the access to global programmes is mostly restricted to more affluent sections of society in view of the cost involved. This may further accentuate the educational inequalities in developing countries; the unequal competition may result in poor performing institutes being swallowed by best performing institutes; (3) development of distance education programmes materials on a global level may be an impossible task and more difficult, which mean the curriculum development in a particular cultural context, or country may not suit another country or a different cultural context; (4) lack in usage of modern technologies and inordinate delay in implementing are also major problems in the distance education institutions in the country like India.

Further, the study suggested following various restructuring measures towards globalization of ODL (1) the distance education institutes in India have to build partnership with the various sectors of the society viz. business, commerce, industry, agriculture, journalism, administrations etc. which would facilitate employment opportunities for all those who get the privilege of pursuing studies in the distance education institutions; (2) in fields such as engineering, management and computer science, industry and distance education institution collaboration is needed which can yield significant benefit for both sides in areas such as curriculum development, equipment donations, usage of laboratory facilities, faculty training, learner's scholarships etc.; (3) every effort has to be made to increase the level of market value as well as the target group of at least 20 per cent from the eligible population during the first decade of twenty first century; (4) the ODL institutions should change the curriculum from time to time enabling learners to convert information into knowledge; and (5) the continuous assessment may be in the form of assignment, closed book test or open book test, problem solving skill, project etc., depending upon the programme.

A study by Seol Jinah (2005) identifies major barriers to the internationalization of traditional higher education and to suggest how they may be targeted as opportunities for open and distance education. Based on the experiences of an online "Cyber University" a functioning university consortium consisting of traditional and open universities in Korea, it provides new perspectives that will enhance collaboration and networking among distance education institutions through regional consortia projects and partnerships. The findings and suggestions are: (1) distance education is becoming one of the booming sectors in the global educational economy; it is likely that the dominant universities worldwide will increasingly focus on expanding their share in the global education market to compensate for diminishing public funding everywhere; (2) the change and challenges facing traditional higher education indicate that new developments in relation to the globalization and internationalization of education must be scrutinized at the institutional and regional levels; (3) as the imperatives of the educational market are now driving internationalization trends worldwide, Asian universities and distance education institutions should also seek to make themselves attractive to overseas students and to build links with universities in other countries to enhance their global reach; and (4) a regional distance education consortium based on virtual community will be a great stepping stone for not only developing transnational education network within Asia but also beyond.

Finally, it is observed that virtual higher education can enable easy access to education and training provisions throughout Asia, and it is important to emphasize increasing virtual mobility, the exchange of learning material, as well as new types of interactivity and flexibility in distance education. Futhermore, it is strongly suggested that joint research and development efforts be formed to enhance the cooperation and competencies of participating universities with regard to virtual learning. Courses and curriculum co-operation in the perspective of large diversity of provisions should also fit the need of regional students and nation state. The virtual school must be attractive to international aspirants and be competitive in content not only in Asia but also internationally.

Consumption Abroad Mode

A study by Altbach (1999) analyzed the aspect of student mobility and highlighted the positive and negative aspects of globalization of higher education. It has been found that more than a million students studying outside their home countries—majority of them from Asia and studying in the United States, Britain, Canada and Australia. In between 1996 to 1998, students going from Korea to the US increased by 15.5 per cent, from India by 10.4 per cent, and from China by 10.5 per cent. Japan, still the largest sending country to the US, increased by just 1.7 per cent and Hong Kong declined by 11.7 per cent. The hosts 4,81,000 overseas students, the large majority of whom pay all of their expenses.

A study by Narag (2001) has analyzed the University of Delhi's efforts to promote its programmes for international students; further it brought out the available facilities for admission to foreign students and the problems faced by the foreign students. The Delhi University has established the "Foreign Students Registry Cell" to carry out admission related activities of foreign students in the university and a provision of reservation of 5 per cent of the total seats has been made in first year of course at the undergraduate level in every college for the international students. University was receiving nearly 550-600 international students; among them approximately 80 per cent enrolment was at the undergraduate level and rest at the Master, M.Phil. and Ph.D. level. And out of total foreign students, nearly 60 per cent were representing from countries like Nepal, Sri Lanka, Bangladesh, Mauritius, Kenya, Uganda, Vietnam and Tibet. On the other hand, major demand for commerce and vocational courses and which is increasing; following other courses like Computers, Basic Sciences, Buddhist Studies and Languages etc.

Further, the study observed following problems faced by overseas students: (a) complex administrative process (formality) of their respective Embassies/High Commissions due to this they arrive after the last date of admission; (b) lack of good accommodation facility (hostel) is another problem. The study argues that University of Delhi was not adopted aggressive marketing strategies for its education services.

A study by Bhalla Veena (2003) utilizing secondary data analyzed the country-wise foreign students inflow to India during 1993-94 to 2001-02 and status of selected Indian universities in attracting foreign students during 2001-02. The mixed and fluctuating trends were observed in students' inflow; the regions viz. South and Central Asia, West Asia and East Africa are sending the largest number of students. There is sharp fall in the students flow from the African countries viz. Kenya, Sudan and Ethiopia; on the contrary, the students from the United States is increasing; it reflects the growing significance of Study Abroad Programmes in the United States. Further, it observed that about twenty seven (27) Indian universities have attracted more than fifty (50) foreign students during 2001-02. The University of Pune (1630), Manipal Academy of Higher Education (1070) and the University of Delhi (1027) were the front runner among other universities in attracting foreign students.

A study by Sharma and Maheshwari (2004) have analyzed current status of student mobility and trade in education; the developed countries viz. USA, UK, Australia, Germany, France and Japan are attracting maximum number of overseas students through their quality education, good infrastructure, good visa support and free trade in education services. The maximum number of students (41%) are going abroad for higher studies from Asian countries followed by Europe. The study highlights changing pattern in international/transnational education services. In this respect developed countries formally declared their interest toward trade in education and they have revised education policies so as to help their education institutions to develop their education market. Australia and UK are capturing more market through their free trade policy. Due to Information and Communication Technology Network Distance Education is expanding in the world and the twinning programmes are getting good attention in developing and underdeveloped countries.

A study by Ahmad (2005) analyzed the international trends of student mobility in higher education. It has been observed from the study that education has treated as 'tradable commodity' in the world; consequently developed countries are taking advantages of it particularly OECD countries viz. (USA, UK, Germany, France, Australia, Canada) account for almost 70 per cent of total tertiary level educational exports in the world and on the other hand, the Asian countries are an important market for higher education. The study briefly glanced over the measures taken by the Government of India for boosting its higher education at international level viz. establishment of Educational Consultants India Ltd. (Ed CIL) as a nodal agency for placement and attracting more and more foreign students in Indian institutions; the District Administration of Students Abroad (DASA) scheme has been launched to encourage international students; on the other hand, an amount of Rs. 1500 crore Technical Education Quality Improvement Programme (TEQIP) has been started to upgrade 150 well performing engineering colleges to world class standards. The UGC has initiated a programme for the Promotion of Indian Higher Education Abroad (PIHEAD).

Finally, the study suggested few actions of implementation to increase India's education market at international level. (a) Globalization of educational services should be seen as an opportunity by Indian universities and higher educational institutions should maintain world standards and establish their bases in other countries; (b) for keeping comprehensive database on students mobility, i.e. inflow and outflow is need of the hour; (c) a proper co-ordination in between UGC, MHRD and Ministry of External Affairs should be maintained; (d) an effective registration and certification system is essential to restrict the entry of substandard institutions and India should target Asian countries for attracting overseas students.

Commercial Presence Mode

A study by Takwale (1998) has made an attempt to find out the five types of foreign providers transactions viz., Formal-Twinning partnership, Distance Education-Twinning partnership, Networked partnership for Distributed Classroom and Networked Partnership for International Education; where the communication technology has predominant role in these five partnership transactions. The study observed the two purposes of the evolving partnership: one is to get the knowledge and expertise necessary for the process of modernization and globalization; and the other is to employ the knowledge for the rapid socio-economic development of the participating countries.

Further, the study identified some major issues in foreign partnerships, viz. (a) assessment of quality and standard of the programmes; (b) recognition of the degree within and outside the country for employment and further admission; (c) ensuring equivalence with the comparable degrees offered in the two countries; (d) comparability for recognition within the country in terms of duration, content, level and coverage of knowledge and skills, competency development needed for professional/vocational courses, etc. (e) reciprocity-allowing each one to offer its course in the other country on the same terms and conditions.

A study by Altbach (1999) found various benefits and challenges of globalization of higher education; on positive side, it serves rapidly growing demand for access to higher education, stimulates cross-national educational innovation, prepares students for work in a global economy and on the other hand, challenges like regulating of Offshore provider and ensuring the quality, worthiness of programme and its charge are matter of concern. Finally, the study pointed out that Internationalization of higher education is a repetition of colonial era and where foreigners are welcomed with open arms. Hence, it is time to stand back and assess the impact of the explosion of foreign higher education models in Asia. The current wave of globalization of higher education brings with it the dangers of total lack of regulation and control. It is a bad idea, in education at least, to permit caveat emptor to dominate.

A study by Dhar and Dhar (2001) has discussed an important regulations for commercial presence mode viz. immigration regulations, exchange controls, non-recognition of equivalent qualifications work as obstacles for consumption abroad and on the other hand, nationality requirements, restrictions on the number of foreign teachers employed, the conditions concerning the use of resources, the existence of public monopolies and subsidies to nation etc. The study observed that the agreements of WTO have changed the traditional methods of education with a multiplicity of new teaching and learning methods, new types of establishments have emerged, providing non-university courses, including part-time courses, evening classes, in-service courses and distance learning; and created much educational opportunities to youths with increasing their rate of participation in higher education. Finally, the study pointed out that, among the emerging trends of "twinning agreements", "franchising" and "distance learning" are becoming increasingly popular.

A similar observation was made by Altbach (1999), that universities/institutions from industrialized countries are increasingly active in offering degrees through Offshore Campus/Twinning Arrangements; but increasingly foreign educational providers are setting up shop in Asia without working with a local educational institution.

A study by Knight (2003) outlined the purpose and rules of GATS with its relevance to higher education and identified some key policy issues which needed to be addressed. The study has raised important questions concerning quality assurance, professional mobility and recognition of qualifications, and considers the issues from the perspectives of both the developed and developing world. Further, the study recognized that trade issues are closely related to the large issues of commercialization and commodification of education but the focus remains on the potential impact of trade rules on cross-border education. More attention is given to the delivery of education/ training courses and programmes across borders (modes 1 and 3) than to the movement of students to study in foreign countries (mode 2). Again, the intention of the study is to take a balanced approach in discussing the implication of new trade rules and increased trade in education services; also potential benefits and risks are identified.

A study by Powar (2004) analyzed the data of foreign education providers' commercial presence in India; and found that in late 2000 there were 27 providers having presence in India and which increased to 61 in 2004; which reveals that Indian market is being increasingly sought by the developed countries. Further, the mechanism of Trade in Higher education in different (four) modes to India and the actions that are required to be taken (regulation/promotional mechanisms) are briefly discussed; the study pointed out that "Of the four modes of trade in services, consumption abroad and presence of natural persons do not pose any serious problem. However, there is a need to regulate commercial presence and to some extent cross border supply through the impact of the latter is presently not clear".

Finally, the study highlighted the importance of domestic regulations in order to prevent the entry of non-accredited universities/ institutions and ultimately safeguarding the nation's interests. The intention behind the regulations are to facilitate collaboration and partnerships between Indian and foreign institutions, systematize the operation of foreign institutions already operating in India; safeguard the interest of the Indian student community; enforce accountability on the part of the foreign providers.

A report prepared by Bhushan (2005) is a research project conducted by the NIEPA, New Delhi. It has provided an overview of the mechanism of operations imparting foreign degrees in different types of institutions in India and it provides global scenario on working of foreign education providers in various countries; with the regulations (guidelines) introduced by the countries viz. Malaysia, China, Singapore, Hong Kong, Australia and New Zealand. Also collects the perception of students and teachers on foreign education providers.

It observed that, majority of the foreign education providers provide professional (vocational) courses and maximum number of programmes is offered under the twinning arrangement by the foreign education providers. Out of the total sample of 131 institutions, 107 were providing for vocational courses, 19 for technical courses and only 5 for general education. The data shows that in the category of vocational courses management courses were the most popular. Business Management and Hotel Management constitute approximately 80 per cent of the total number of courses. Further, it found that, foreign education providers do not prefer collaborate with public and non-profit institutions and the collaborative courses are more skill-oriented and communication-oriented rather than their emphases on research. But there is no standard setting mechanism for the foreign educational institutions causing concern to the stakeholders; however there are some aspects of good practices such as flexibility of curriculum design, credit transfer facility, job placement, multiple entry and multiple exit system, etc., and need to be followed by public institutions in higher education. On the question of "accreditation of the courses" affecting the students' decision to pursue the course, it was found that for 59 per cent of the students it hardly mattered and only 41 per cent were of the opinion that it did matter to them.

The study has made following recommendations: (1) need for a Regulatory Body to register, approve and monitor the overall operation of foreign education providers in India; (2) priority areas for collaboration should be finalized and need to develop institution to check quality; (3) no objection from Embassy should be compulsory; (4) demand and supply chain in higher education must balance as per the priority of a country; (5) trade-based internationalization of higher education leading to commercialization must be checked; (6) there should be mutual recognition of the degrees by respective countries as well; (7) there should be a database on all aspects of the foreign education providers and the students should be completely informed about the foreign institutions; (8) NAAC should be allowed to accredit foreign programmes and examine the academic creditworthiness of foreign institutions. NAAC's evaluation of quality should be taken into account before allowing foreign institutions to operate in India.

A study by Usha Devi (2011) brought out various issues and implications of foreign universities in India; the study has observed following implications that: (1) if foreign universities are set up with the intention to reap economic gains, it would lead to commodification of higher education and it defeats the very purpose of higher education; (2) these universities would only be preparing workforce for low end or middle level jobs in a market driven economy; (3) India can partially arrest (brain drain) the outflow of students to foreign universities at abroad and Indian neo-rich and middle class students may benefit; (4) as the social inclusion and justice is concerned, the entry of foreign universities will further accentuate the disparities hitting hard the marginalized section of the society; (5) these universities are likely to create separate islands and enclaves within the already stratified Indian higher education system; (6) they may create high flying life of a student in their campus and fee structure of foreign universities will be higher than the host universities; (7) student community might be switch-over from 'studying abroad' to study in foreign universities in India; (8) foreign universities might be able to tap the working professionals in the sunrise sector.

A study by Bhattacharya Joyati (2012) observed that, due to adoption of internationalization will emerge lot of operational challenges; cultural dissimilarity and unfamiliarity with local market condition will complicate the situation. This problem is categorized as 'information asymmetry' which occurs when entities from entirely different markets creep in the system. Besides, in the absence of any world class university, internationalization will be a one-way traffic in case of India in which Indian students will move in large number to foreign countries without any reciprocation on the other side.

The study expressed concern about the negligence in the core areas of knowledge viz. mathematics, physics, literature, arts will lead losing the current hold of Indian professionals at the international level in the long run; the worrying is that in terms of research and the purely academic disciplines India is beginning to trail in comparison not just to other universities but its own past performance. Finally, suggested several remedies to Indian higher education system (1) reforming of education and uniform standard of education at school and the college level should be introduced; (2) more autonomy should have to be granted to the institutions of higher learning with a mechanism of further decentralization so that they can devise new techniques of excellence; (3) there is also an urgency to review the university acts in different states and revise the same in the light of the new requirements and the challenges being faced by the state universities; (4) a less clumsy regulatory framework has to be evolved to give direction to the much debated and controversial move towards privatization; (5) proper steps must be formulated so that inclusion is not done at the cost of academic standard.

International Branch Campuses

In studying the cycle of business education in Malaysia, Qureshi and Luqmani (2008) proposed several business strategies for transnational education providers to enhance their branches competitiveness. Firstly, home institutions need to make affordability a priority before branch campuses are launched. Tuition, housing subsidies and scholarships are areas that can potentially reduce cost; (2) home institutions need to tailor courses to local demand in host countries. For foreign partners, accreditations, clear benchmarks and regular monitoring need to be established for ongoing improvement and enhancing classroom activities; (3) branches need to place emphasis on screening faculty credentials, offering better pay and more manageable teaching loads to ensure faculty long-term teaching commitment in a host country; (4) well-planned faculty training rather than *ad hoc* training is desired; lastly, to get alumni and employers inputs are all possible approaches to advertise branches; they involved in the recruiting, curriculum design and career development process and it is also important to use online tools, such as blogs and chats sites become influential discussion forums for students in deciding the branch they choose.

A study by Becker (2010) analyzed the market trends of international branch campuses in the globe; the study observed following trends: (1) since September 2006, the number of international branch campuses in the world have increased by 43 per cent, to 162 and more source and host countries have become involved in branch-campus development; (2) institutions from the United States dominated, both in the number of established operations and in the campus growth over the past three years; (3) seventy-eight campuses, the equivalent of 48 per cent of all current international branch campuses, have been set up by US institutions. The US is followed by Australia (14 campuses), the UK (13) and France and India (11) campuses, each; (4) among the host countries, the United Arab Emirates (UAE) is the clear leader, hosting 40 international branch campuses, a quarter of all such ventures in the world. Two-thirds of these foreign campuses are located in Dubai International Academic City. China is in second position among the host countries, with 15 campuses, followed by Singapore (12) and Qatar (9 campuses); (5) recently, the directions of branch-campus establishment have started to change. Developing countries are slowly but increasingly establishing their own branch campuses abroad. It is due to improved quality of higher education programmes in developing countries; (6) the international branch-campus market has become more competitive hence the institutions should undertake careful market research before deciding to create a campus abroad.

Further, the study pointed out various factors which are responsible for increase in the number of international branch campuses: (a) a high student demand, coupled with the country's need to build a knowledge economy; (b) few host countries viz. Singapore and Qatar are actively trying to establish themselves as "International Higher Education Hubs" for their region; (c) host countries are inviting, providing support, funding, or infrastructure to foreign providers.

A study by Altbach (2010) has specified a number of unpredictable factors that prevent a branch campus from sustaining: (a) branch campuses are not really campuses, but rather small and specialized academic programmes, such as business management and information technology which require low set up cost and have great worldwide demand; (b) the lack of commitment of professors from the home institution to teach in host countries may pose the biggest challenge to sustainability; (c) branches often offer a limited range of academic programmes, it is difficult for students to gain real educational experience that replicates that of home campuses; (d) in a host country where an increasing number of branch campuses and local universities compete with each other, it may be difficult to sustain the conventional model of only accepting host country students who meet stringent selection criteria set by home institutions, particularly for prestigious institutions which have high enrollment standards; and (e) local conditions make the long-term outcomes of branch campuses unpredictable. Branch campuses may be less attractive in China in the near future given the expanding local capacity at all levels. The study pointed out that long term future market for branch campuses is difficult to predict. Further, it suggested that, sustainability should be a central concern when establishing a branch campus, but there is little evidence of such a concept.

A study by Naidov Vik (2010) discussed following four rationales to explain in growth in transnational higher education; these rationales are derived from research undertaken by the organization for Economic Cooperation and Development, Centre for Educational Research and Innovation: (1) the mutual understanding rationale[5] emphasizes academic, cultural social and political grounds for the internationalization of education and does not consider education as part of an articulated economic policy; (2) under the skilled migration rationale[6], internationalization is meant to attract foreign students who then encouraged to stay in the source country post-graduation and contribute its knowledge economy; (3) the revenue generation rationale[7] highlights the market and trade approach of transnational higher education. It reflects income as an important rationale for recruiting international students; (4) lastly the capacity development rationale views transnational higher education as a means of fulfilling the unmet demand for education from local constituents and building capacity and capability for quality education. These four rationales for the growth of transnational higher education are not mutually exclusive. For example: a source country might benefit from revenue generation, while the receiving country is promoted through capacity and capability building.

A study by Shollapur (2010) has analyzed the impact of FDI on Indian higher education system: (1) the entry of foreign universities will indeed enhance educational opportunities in India and it will provide greater access to quality education for Indian students; which would curtail a large outflow of Indian students travelling to the US and Europe in search of quality education.; (2) FDI in higher education would help in imparting an international perspective to the contents of the curriculum; (3) the course offering would be governed by the prevalent market forces that have enough potential in preparing graduates as required by contemporary recruiters. The employment potentiality of a course/programme not only attracts students but also generates enough revenue to the offering institutions; (4) it would accelerate the global mobility of teachers in particular and would bring together international faculty under a single roof; it would greatly benefit the students of the host country; (5) the competition between the domestic and international universities/institutes would improve their quality, efficiency and accountability. Further, the study suggested that appropriate measures need to be initiated for retaining bright faculty in domestic universities/institutes; hence, there is a need to ponder over the current preparedness and action plans of the domestic institutions in combating the competition from the foreign universities.

A study by Yi Cao (2011) focused on offshore institutions; it discussed definitions, challenges of institutional sustainability, as well as strategies for sustaining offshore operations. The study found that demand for cross-border education branch campuses have become an important form of delivery in the Asia and Pacific region; most recent branch campuses were built to generate revenue, much of the research on branch campuses focuses on business strategies. Further, the study suggested that, future research also needs to be done to explore strategies above and beyond a business model to reflect the intrinsic value of higher education serving the public good.

Marketization

A study by Prasad (2001) pointed out that the marketization of higher education is considered to be better than complete privatization. This involves allowing market forces to determine the need for setting up of institutions, the hiring of faculty, the choice of course of study, the methods of teaching etc. Further, it suggested for encouragement to private bodies under the guidance of the government and specialized agencies.

A study by Tilak (2004) has offered an analytical account of some of the prominent emerging trends in higher education and described how higher education is moving from state to market, and the costs involved therein; further it gives a quick review of some of the arguments being made in favour of the state versus markets and restated how important it is for the state to continue to play a critical role in higher education. It is argued that any significant reduction in the role of the state in higher education is neither feasible, nor desirable.

The study observed that the march towards marketization of higher education is taking place through a variety of measures: financial privatization of public universities, transfer of ownership of public institutions, and establishment of private institutions—private institutions with government support, self-financing private institutions (with government support), and profit-making private institutions—all focusing on short term market considerations and immediate market relevance; it indicates that the Government is encouraging higher education institutions to adopt market relevant policies. Further, study stated that any attempt to build a partnership between the public-private in education (middle path-state market partnership) may be counter-productive. Under state market partnership the market forces is tremendous and once set freed, these forces cannot be easily controlled and consequently the middle path state-market partnership ultimately converges with the total market system. Similar observation made by another author discussing the pros and cons of privatization of higher, is the newly emerging trend of marketization will successfully be able to combine the goals of equity and quality? He suggested that the huge investment in higher education can be met only through an appropriate and healthy Public-Private Partnership (PPP) model (Bhattacharya Joyati, 2012). The study strongly supported the public subsidization to higher education, but universalization of public subsidization to higher education may produce adverse effects, therefore, the solution to regressive effects of subsidies lies in progressive taxation system, rather in eliminating or reducing subsidies.

A study by Pawar Sanjay (2010) analyzed the marketing of higher education through Off-shore campuses; it brought out the importance of marketing strategies for off-shore campuses by identifying following strategies: (1) advertising through print media in both home and host countries; (2) spot or strip advertising on TV in the host country; (3) participating in international educational fairs/exhibitions; (4) creating dedicated websites for international viewing. Further, it observed that the success of off-shore centres is depending on the strategies adopted for marketing and professional approach involving systematic planning, monitoring of the requirements of students, interactive sessions guided by senior academics and personalized attention is required.

Issues for Research

From the foregoing review of literature, the following important research issues have been identified. As evident from the review of literature that no satisfactory analysis has been done mode-wise implication of higher education service in the context of India. There are few studies available analyzing the globalization and internationalization of higher education. From the policy viewpoint intensive analysis of mode-wise implication is much required to face the eventualities of WTO. Student Mobility is the oldest phenomena of internationalization of higher education in the context of India; there is hardly any study examining the students' inflow and outflow during pre- and post-WTO period under various dimensions and identifying the nature of, continent-wise, country-wise, size of, reasons of, source of mobility; hence it is another important issue for research. As regarding the overall development of higher education under different dynasty and rulers to till WTO regime is another issue of research which has been analyzed in the study under one roof; further problems of the higher education system are identified.

Depending upon the availability of data and resources, the following important research issues have been identified for analysis in the present study. GATS article-wise implication of higher education in India is analyzed and mode-wise trade in higher education services have been presented in the study; further the study identify the policy measures to optimize the opportunities and minimize the challenges of GATS agreements. The present study has modestly attempted to cover some of these research gaps identified above under the given data constraint.

Notes

1. There are various stages of education like Primary, Secondary, Higher Secondary and Higher education.

2. The New Economic Policy was initiated during 1991, under this Liberalizations, Privatization and Globalization (LPG) measures are undertaken.
3. Internationalization of higher education refers to the specific policies and initiative of countries and individual academic institutions or systems to deal with global trends (Altbach, 2002).
4. Globalization of higher education means the trends in higher education that have cross-national implications, including mass higher education and a global market place for students, faculty and highly educated personnel as well as the global reach of the new interest-based technologies (Altbach, 2002).
5. Under mutual understanding concept, the internationalization policies for higher education are based on strengthening ties between countries through the creation of networks of political and business elites (Naidov Vik, 2010).
6. Skilled migration approach is more devoted to bringing students to the source country rather than taking transnational programmes to receiving countries (Naidov Vik, 2010).
7. Some traditional receiving counties have in recent years, shown an interest in developing their transnational delivery to take advantage of the export revenues thus provided to the internationalization of education. Singapore is key example of this strategy (Naidov Vik, 2010).

3

Development of Higher Education in India

A Brief Historical Perspective and Present Status

Introduction

The role of education in nation building is really exemplary and it is a basic input for building knowledge society; the continuous acquisition and expansion of knowledge is not merely advantageous, but it has become inevitable in globalized world. It is obvious that, the growth and prosperity of individual and nation depend upon approach of universities and system of education. Because universities are the highest and the most sacred social institutions of nation, indeed there we educate our future elite. It is passionate of Radhakrishnan, the university is not merely academic; but actively constructive as well which helps to build a robust and vibrant country; in fact richness of nation lies in quality outcome from universities which is real strength and growth of nation.

Since ancient period, the various factors such as political, religious and administrative had influenced and changed the India's indigenous education; as a result of this it has become a comprehensive and complex system. At this juncture, studying the originality of Indian education system and its development is necessary to understand it and to introduce suitable changes for bringing competence and relevance; further it may lead to an assessment of various issues and problems of higher education in globalized era.

Historical Perspective

Various periods of the country's history viz., the Hindu period, the period of Buddhist, early period of Muhammadan and Mughal, and British periods, nurtured and influenced India's indigenous education. In each of these periods, there was a specific addition to the indigenous system of education. Furthermore, the educational progress was deeply affected by the country's political events. Nevertheless education was kept alive because of the people's support and in the last resort; it was the private sector that came to the rescue of learning. During the British rule, the modern education was introduced, which was an event of great historical significance for India. In those days, mainly three important agencies were responsible for the spread of modern education in India, viz. the Foreign Christian Missionaries, the British Government and the Progressive Indians. As a matter of fact, India has all along been a colourful and magnificent country with great religious movements, rich and ancient languages vast store of literature and many strings of arts and architecture. Hence, it is desirable to know the background of the country, the people and their education in order to comprehend the problems of education in India. For the convenience of the study, the whole period of Indian history is broadly divided into four parts i.e., Ancient India, Medieval period, British rule and lastly the Post-independence era.

A. Education System in Ancient India

Ancient education was mainly the studying of Vedas which consisted of in the perfect acquirement of the text through Koss and the work of Aryabhatta, Panini, Katyayana, Kautilya, Patanjali and Medical treatise of Charaka and Susruta belonging to the mass of literature of this period. It is said that in the early Vedic period education was considered as of family responsibility, the father being the educator of his children. Such a principle did not facilitate the growth of large educational institutions which became obstacle for spreading of education among the masses. But institutionalized education had developed almost by the later Vedic period and the age of Upanishads.

In the early Vedic period, education consisted of learning to recite the holy text, pupils were going to some teacher for education, and the home of the teacher was functioning as school. And very intimate relationship was observed between students and their teachers as members of the same family. No fee was charged. The students were, required to help the teacher in his family and farm work in his additional time. After completion of studentship, usually at twelve years, lastly pupils could start some very specialized study of a subject or specific problem and approach some renowned teacher of the subject and learn under his guidance. Here the duration of the course was neither fixed, nor was it compulsory to take under such a course.

By all accounts, Brahmins alone had the privilege to study all higher religious and secular education among the Hindus. As Desai A.R. (2004) observed, "The Brahmin enjoyed the monopoly of all higher education. Further, this education, as a part of the entire culture of the Hindu society, controlled and administered by the Brahmins". Professional education was carried on the basis of hereditary, it was a creative era characterized by the development of metaphysics, philology, grammar, astronomy, mathematics, medicine, metallurgy and of philosophic and political thought. About specialization in different branches was concerned, started and values of new discoveries were realized. Later came Jainism and Buddhism with their emphasis upon the system of organized brotherhood accommodated in the rock cut halls, Viharas and Monastries. Similar to this the Brahmanical system followed with institutions like 'Mathas' and regular colleges, as we know. Whatever institutions, therefore, gradually marched to glory or fame were the creation of private teachers, the specialist and their devoted pupils. Indeed, during Vedic period, the only private teacher was schooling in his house, creating it as the educational institution.

During Buddhist Period, education was made available to all who sought to have it without any restriction. Those who had previously been deprived of education were now bidden to come and learn. The sense of equality that flowered forth in liberalism found expression in further changes. Buddhist monks were drawn from all sections of society. The classes conducted in Buddhist Monasteries, known as Viharas, were open to both Buddhists and non-Buddhists alike. Hindu temple colleges were started in South India at about 8th century.

The organization of Buddhist education system got further stability as a result of elaborate residential and other arrangements. Originally, the monk did not have any dwelling house properly so called. Takshasila, Nalanda and Vikramshila Universities were some of the centres of higher education during this period. Nalanda was a worldwide acclaimed university of that time and students from foreign countries used to come and gain knowledge here. It had trained scholars and knowledge was imparted on almost all subjects including science, philosophy, medicine, welfare etc., but Mathematical as well as the Astronomical department was quite renowned. To get admission in university students had to clear a very tough entrance examination. In fact Nalanda was the first university in the world to have given Astronomy a separate status from Mathematics. It is said that the library of Nalanda University contained invaluable books belonging to a wide range of topics (http://www.indiansaga.inf/others/nalanda.html).

It is evident that during this period, the aims of education were similar to those of Vedic age. But instead of emphasizing spiritual height, the stress now was on development of moral character which included among other things, sweetness of disposition, right conduct, integrity, morality, piety and virtue in the daily life of individual. Another observation is that, since 6th century B.C. student mobility is proceeding for acquiring higher knowledge throughout the world. It is found that, "Buddhist monasteries developed into corporate educational institutions, and some like Nalanda, Valabhi and Vikramshila became international centres of learning (Biswas, A. and Agrawal, S.P., 1994)". Further, it has been observed from the statement given by Fahien and Hiuen Tsang about the Nalanda University is enough evidence that the Indians had attained the great proficiency in the field of education.

When Buddhism began to decay, the Hinduism tried to overpower it by reaching larger masses of people and opening more centres of learning, big and small, at innumerable places all-over the country. Since Neo-Brahmanism was only a revival of the old Brahmanical religion which was adapted to the changed needs of the time, the concept of education did not undergo change from what it had been described in the Vedic period. As more people desired education under the impact of new religion, some seats of learning were started by organizations that covered a larger area through their activities. Such expansion of education stood in need of large finances and more elaborate system of financing the institutions.

B. Education System During Medieval Period

In this period the early Muhammadan rulers and the succeeding Mughal rulers brought changes in the Ancient Indian education. The promotion of education was mainly dependent upon individual character of ruler. For a time the indigenous system of education was deprived of royal support and patronage which was now directed to the promotion of the new Islamic learning. Consequently, its development far from being steady and continuous was uneven and weak. A well-developed popular system of education was not existed during the Muhammadan and the Mughal period.

Among the Muslim rulers, Sultan Muhammad Ghori, was the first king of India who deemed it as his duty to impart education on somewhat definite bases. At Ajmer he set up some schools and seminaries for the spread of Islamic culture, and learning in that province. The successors of the slave Kings like Qutab-ud-din-Aibak, Iltutmish, Raziyya and Balban were all patrons of learning. Qutab-ud-din Aibak was a man of literary tastes proficient in Persian and Arabic. He promoted Muhammadan learning by raising mosques which were centres of both religion and learning. The slave kings were succeeded by the Khilji dynasty which stepped into the throne of Delhi. Ala-ud-Din-Khilji, a remarkable ruler of this dynasty was an enthusiastic friend of learning.

After the disintegration of Khiljis, Muslim education was promoted by the new dynasty which was known as Tughaluq dynasty. Firuz Shah Tughaluq was greatly contributed to the material, cultural and educational welfare of subjects viz. history, art and archaeology. Encouraging learned men for imparting education to the people was the important part of his state policy and in his reign both Hindus and Mohammadans were learning each other's languages.

Babar, the memorable founder of the Mughal Empire, was a great scholar in Arabic, Persian and Turk. Biswas A. and Agrawal S.P. (1994) study regarding Babar's work on education observed that, Babar entrusted his Public Works Department with the additional duty of conducting postal service, the publication of a Gazette and the building of schools and colleges. It indicates that establishment of educational institutions were considered an important aspect of administration. Babar encouraged higher education by grants of land/money to the mosques, monasteries and stipends to individual saints and scholars. Babar was succeeded by his son, Humayun who was a great bibliophile and a studious scholar. He built a madrasah at Delhi, of which Shaikh Husain was a professor. In his period, private individuals built few schools and colleges. There are two examples of educational institutions founded by private individuals—a college near Chunar and a school near Agra (Biswas A. and Agrawal S.P., 1994).

At the time of Akbar education received a great impetus. His uncommon thirst for knowledge prompted him to build the famous

Ibadat Khana where learned men of every faith held intellectual debates and fearless public discussions. Akbar built colleges at Fatehpur Sikkri and other places. During his period vast impetus was given to original research and scholarship, and authorship was rewarded with magnificent allowances. Akbar introduced innovations and improvements in the educational system, modes of study and curriculum. Educational institutions were multiplied, even private individuals promoted the cause of education by establishing schools and colleges, including the famous madrasah built by Maham Anga, the wet-nurse of Akbar. It was observed from the work of Akbar that he treated both Muslims and Hindus equally in his period. He gave whole-hearted protection to Hindu learning; caused the translations of Hindu classics and scriptures like Mahabharata, Ramayana, Atharva-Veda, Leelavati and Panchatantra into Persian; and provided the education of Hindus in their own culture in madrasahs along with the Muslims, eager as he was to further the education of both the communities alike (Biswas A. and Agrawal S.P., 1994).

Shah Jahan, a cultured king and a refined scholar, made a distinct contribution by funding an Imperial College at Delhi and repaired the college, named Dar-ul-Baga which had been almost in ruins. Later on, Aurangzab founded numerous schools and colleges in his kingdom and never neglected his duty with regard to education of his subjects in the outlying provinces that acknowledged his suzerainty. During Bahadur Shah-I rule, two colleges were established in Delhi—one founded by Ghaziuddin near Ajmeri Gate and the other by Khan Firuz Jang.

Higher education or education in general did not get the attention as it received in ancient India. Besides, the political climate that proved unfavourable or otherwise for education, the attitude of emperors toward Hindu education and the measures adopted by them, decided the course of this system and the demand for Hindu education did not grow during this period, only few rulers of this time protected Hindu education. Besides being deprived of the state support, it brought no gains by way of securing high offices of favour of the princes and kings. The Brahmins struck to their old faith and fewer scholars went to them for knowledge. Higher class Hindus started joining Persian schools, which gave a further hindrance to higher learning during the period. Thus, it was obvious that the demand for Muslim education was confined to a minor part of the population and demand for Hindu learning decreased considerably on account of the attitude of the rulers and change in state religion and language.

C. Development of Education During the British Rule in India

The British East India Company came in 1600 to India for trading concern, which soon followed, added to the western element in Indian education. The East India Company had strong ambition of establishing an empire in India; consequently it emerged as victors by the middle of 18th century. Obliviously they rose to be rulers and education had their responsibility. Incidentally, the Foreign Christian Missionaries entered India to provide western education to Indian masses, they did extensive work in the sphere of the modern education in India, and their principal aim in starting educational institutions was religious i.e. spreading of Christianity among the Indian people. It was in this manner that Western education came to prevail in India. Thus, with the entry of Westerners in India, the political system of the country took a different shape and at the same time the organization of educational institutions also deviated from its earlier course. The East India Company was, however, the principal agent in disseminating modern western education in India. The introduction of western education in India was primarily motivated by the political-administrative and economic needs of Britain in India. They required a large number of educated individuals, who would staff the administrative machinery of the British rule. Thus, it became necessary to establish schools and colleges in India.

The Charter Act of 1813 marked a point of departure in the East India Company towards the education of its Indian subjects. Under it, the company, for the first time, assumed State responsibility for education. It provided that 'a sum of not less than a lakh of rupees in each year shall be set apart and applied to the revival and improvement of literature and encouragement of learned natives of India and for the introduction and promotion of a knowledge of the science among the inhabitants of the British territories in India for educational purposes. This clause in the Act of 1813 can be cited as an important landmark in the history of development of Western education in India.

Lord Macaulay, the first law member of the Governor General's Executive Council, was responsible for giving specific shape of the British educational policy in India, realizing the importance of the

English medium and Western learning for India's progress, he laid down a famous minutes about the education policy and submitted it to the then Governor General, William Bentinck in 1835. Being an agreement with Macaulay's views Lord William Bentinck accepted his resolution. Consequently, it was clearly stated that the aim of the Government was the introduction of modern education through the medium of English language.

But, Sir Charles Wood's Dispatch of 1854, which resolved all controversies of the period around the subject of education into well defined attitudes and it initiated a further great march in modernizing Indian education. It put forward a new era in the growth of Western education that was to suggest that with the government sponsoring the scheme in each province, there should be a Department of Public Instruction. The 'dispatch' made an important provision i.e. universal education from Primary to the University levels, consequently the British Indian Government rose in the discharge of its responsibility for the people's welfare. Further, the Dispatch declared that grant-in-aid to be given to private colleges on certain conditions such as stability in management, imparting of good secular education etc.

The first three Universities were established in 1857 and their sole function was to conduct examination, namely "Entrance" examination (after 10 years schooling) and three more college examinations each after two years called respectively 'Licentiate', 'Bachelors' and 'Master's Degrees'. However, the colleges were subordinate to the Universities and the Universities did not undertake any responsibility for teaching.

Indian Education Commission (1882)

In the year 1882 first Indian Education Commission was appointed by Lord Curzon under the chairmanship of Sir William Hunter, the purpose of the commission was to review the existing system of grant-in-aid and the enquiry into the spread of primary education. The Commission made several important suggestions like following of liberal grant-in-aid system to encourage private enterprises in education; Commission wanted a proper combination of private and public efforts from the primary to the university level. It recommended the government to gradual withdrawal from establishment and running of institutions in the sphere of higher education. Further, it stated that the aid to each college be decided after assessing the staff strength, expenditure on maintenance, quality and efficiency etc.

The Commission also recommended the diversification and vocationalization of secondary education and extension of free studentship, facilities to capable students for studies abroad, the education of girls, the education of the backward classes etc. As a result of Commission's recommendation, Indian Private Enterprises received all encouragement for running educational institutions.

The Calcutta University Commission (1917-1919)

The appointment of Commission under the Chairmanship of Michael Sadler (the Sadler Commission) was a landmark in higher education of the country in the year 1917 to enquire into the problems of Calcutta University. The recommendations of the Commission had profoundly influenced on the subsequent progress of higher education throughout the country.

The Commission suggested that teaching Universities should confine themselves to teaching and examining at the degree stages only and high school and intermediate education should be left to the Education Boards which should control education and hold examinations up to the intermediate stage. It also suggested that a number of Teaching Universities should be established to look after higher education. Measures were laid down by the Commission to promote education for women, as also for the professional and vocational training. Again it advocated greater participation of teachers in the governance of Universities, the appointment of full-time Vice-Chancellors and a closer interaction between the Universities and Colleges.

The Government of India issued a resolution in January, 1920, summarizing the Report of the Calcutta University Commission and recommending to the other provisional Governors as well. But majority of the Universities refused to part with their high schools and intermediate examinations except the Allahabad University and the newly formed Dacca University. The Universities of Bombay, Madras and Punjab paid no attention to the recommendation, but Calcutta University followed its teaching. The effect of the Sadler Report on Madras University is seen in a Resolution of the Senate in October, 1920. The results of the Sadler's Commission are best seen in the University for which it was primarily and indeed exclusively meant: Calcutta. The Commission's findings, however, exercised a great influence on the development of higher education in the country.

The Montague-Chelmsford Reforms Act

According to the Montague-Chelmsford Reforms Act, the subjects of administration were divided into two categories i.e., 'Reserved' and 'Transferred'. The 'Reserved' subjects were put under the Provincial Governor and his Executive Council, and 'Transferred' subjects under the Ministers who were responsible to the Provincial Legislature, in respect of developing self-Government had now come into force, and as education was one of the subjects transferred to the control of the elected Legislature, education became a transferred subject under this arrangement and as such the development of education, including University Education, was the responsibility of the Provincial Ministries.

The control which the Central Government exercised over Provincial Government with regard to education more or less lessened. Subsequently, the Government of India Act of 1935 introduced complete provincial autonomy and entrusted the Ministers of Education with greater powers than enjoyed by them under the 1919 Act. The functions of the Government of India in the field of education were of an extremely limited character under this Act.

In accordance with the Government Resolution of 1913, a concern for raising the standard of work in affiliated colleges was felt. This was counted for by the fact that the number of Universities had to increase so that each province could have its own University with jurisdiction extending on further than the boundaries of the province. Within a few years of its being passed, Universities began to increase in numbers. Among the few ones that came into being were the Banaras Hindu University (1916), University of Mysore (1916), Patna University (1917), Osmania University of Hyderabad (1918), Aligarh Muslim University (1920) and University of Lucknow (1920). With this increase in numbers there was a felt need for coordination. To achieve this end, the Inter University Board was set up in 1924.

By the time of 1935, Gandhi had evolved the concept of Basic Education which aimed at solving the problems of education in this country. It was hoped that the ministries in the provinces might get a chance to implement this scheme of education in their respective provinces. Unfortunately, Gandhi's aim could not be achieved due to the Second World War, and the provincial administration was handed over to the nominated advisors of the provincial Governors. The development of education visualized by this scheme would involve a heavy expenditure of public funds, but this was a problem not for the educationists but for those responsible for the Government of the country. Developments since the publication of this report have largely followed the suggestions made by it.

Progress of Education During 1921-1937 A.D.

A satisfactory improvement and expansion in University education took during this period. The establishment of Inter University Board was felt essential to maintain the harmony and mutual co-operation among the universities; and to bring about uniformity and co-ordination in the working of different universities. The Board added five new universities, provision of research facilities and some National Universities into higher education system. The Calcutta University Commission had emphasized its need. The Congress of the Universities of the British Empire held in 1921 and the Bytton Committee constituted for the benefit of Indian students in England had also supported the idea of its establishment. The first All India Conference of Indian Universities was held at Simla in 1924 and an Inter University Board was established.

The Board had representatives of all Universities. After its establishment, the Board solved many intricate and significant problems pertaining to university education. Its annual meetings were held at different educational centres. Besides these meetings a quinquennial conference of the Board was also held in order to provide solution for problems about higher education. It published 'A Hand Book of Indian Universities' which was very important to provide a close knowledge about the working of Indian Universities. Providing information to Indian students about Foreign Universities and to assist Indian Universities in obtaining reorganization for their degrees in other countries was one of the important functions of the Board.

According to the policy of establishing at least one University in each province and from the viewpoint of residential Universities, five new Universities were established during this period viz., Delhi (1922), Nagpur (1923), Andhra (1926), Agra (1927) and Annamalai (1929). Besides the establishment of these Universities some improvements were introduced in the older existing university also during this period. The constitution of Madras University was revised in 1923 and 1929. According to the amendment it developed as a following University. The Bombay University was recognized in 1928 as a result of which facilities for higher education and research work were increased. During this period, the number of affiliated colleges and number of facilities in Universities were increased. As regard the number of affiliated colleges it raised from 201 in 1922 to 466 in year 1937.

The Hartog Report

In May 1928, a Committee was set up under the Chairmanship of Sir Philip Hartog to enquire into the growth of education in British India and potentialities for its further progress. The Committee stated that, the universities and colleges overburdened with too large number of students and the indiscriminate expansion had led to a great deterioration in standards. Further, Committee strongly criticized the Government, because of its act breakup with education.

In 1943, Government of India asked Sir John Sargent, the then Educational Adviser to the Government to prepare a Memorandum of Post-war Education Development in India. As a result, the Sargent Report was published in 1944, it stated that India had the lowest position in university education considering its total population as compared to other countries like Germany, the U.K., the U.S.A., the U.S.S.R. etc. Further the Report had also recommended the institution of an all-India body, a University Grant Committee, under the control of the Central Government, for unifying and coordinating the activities of the different universities, to avoid overlapping and to exercise a general supervision over the allocation of grants to Universities for public funds.

In the year 1945, the University Grants Committee was established, but to begin with it dealt solely with the three Central Universities of Aligarh, Banaras and Delhi, later in 1946-47 it was empowered to deal with all Universities in the country. But this Committee could not prove to be very effective as it was only a recommendatory body with no funds at its disposal. Consequently, at the end of the British period strengthening and enlarging Central responsibility for higher educational development again gained momentum.

Brief of Landmark of Education Policies/Commissions/ Committees

Since pre-independence period, higher education of the country has been guided and influenced by the recommendations and suggestions of various Committees, Boards and Commissions. Hence, it is necessary to glance over various Committees, Boards and Commissions to know the development of education in the country. In this connection, Table 3.1 provides the brief outlook on the development of education policies/commissions/committees in the country.

Table 3.1: Landmarks of Education Policy

Pre-1780 - Ancient India		*Mostly Religious, Excellent Universities, like Nalanda, Vikramshila, etc.*
1781	First Educational Minute of Governor General, Lord Warren	To promote growth and promotion of liberal education in India in first of the college (Madarasa) established in Calcutta, funding of Institutions of Higher education through different Agencies.
1813	Charter Act	Foundation of English Educational system in India. Called for encouragement of learning by "natives of India", and promotion of knowledge of sciences in India. Stress was on Learning English.
1835	Minute of Lord Macaulay	Recommended teaching of English in place of oriental learning to produce English knowing people useful to East India Company; specifically advised that the Indians should be given "what was good for their health and not what was palatable to their taste"; also recommended codification of Hindu and Muslim laws; the British East India Company adopted a resolution accepting the recommendation of Lord Macaulay; this was the first educational declaration; promotion of western arts and sciences was treated as avowed objective of the new policy. This laid the foundation of English Education in the country.
1854	Wood's Despatch	*Magna Carta* of English Education in India. On the recommendations of it, three Universities of Madras, Bombay and Calcutta came to be established in 1857 on the model of London University.
1882-83	First Education Commission during the time of Lord Rippon (Also known as Hunter Commission).	Investigated into the educational developments since 1984, and recommended expansion of education, particularly elementary education and female education. Two other universities were founded at Lahore (1882) and Allahabad (1887).

(*Contd.*)

Table 3.1: *(Contd.)*

Pre-1780 - Ancient India		*Mostly Religious, Excellent Universities, like Nalanda, Vikramshila, etc.*
1902	Indian Universities Commission appointed by Lord Curzon-Raleigh Commission.	Investigated into the status of universities established till then, courses of studies and methods of examination; proposals for new universities and; scholarships and hostel facilities for students also recommended.
1904	University Act	University Act of 1904 was later passed. Conditions of Affiliation were laid down in the Act. This was a great setback to higher education.
1917	Calcutta University Commission	Need of developing linkages between Secondary and University Education, Starting of Honours courses, posts of Professional Readers created, New Universities were set up.
1919	Indian Act	Creation of Inter-University Board, Creation of New Universities, Changes in the Old University Acts, Research Activities, etc. New Universities like BHU, Lucknow University, Patna University, Aligarh Muslim University were set up between 1917-1922.
1929	Hartog Committee	Reported on the quality and status of teachers; condemned hasty expansion of educational institutions; recommended consolidation and improvement.
1935	Government of India Act, 1935	Provincial Autonomy, Educational activities were categorized into federal and provincial subjects, large scale expansion of higher education.
1948-49	Indian Education Commission under the Chairmanship of Dr. Radhakrishnan	Advised expansion and improvement in university education to support the then existing and future requirements of the country; recommended professional education particularly in the field of agriculture, engineering, technology, law, medicine, Teaching days 180, Post-graduate Training and Research, Rural Universities Women's Education setting-up of UGC in 1953.
1958-59	Durgabai Deshmukh Committee on Women's Education.	Emphasised special education facilities for adult and rural women.
1964-66	Education Commission (Kothari Commission)	Recommended a national policy; suggested use of Regional language as medium of Instruction, University autonomy, made comprehensive recommendations on educational reconstruction in all States and sectors; this led to the National

(Contd.)

Table 3.1: (*Contd.*)

Pre-1780 - Ancient India		*Mostly Religious, Excellent Universities, like Nalanda, Vikramshila, etc.*
		Education Policy of 1968; recommendations included uniform educational structure of 10+2+3, common school system, universalization of elementary education, vocationalization of education, etc. Exchange of teachers with other countries.
1986	National Policy on Education, 1986 and POA, 1986	Recommended establishment of a national system of education; emphasized universalization of elementary education, streamlining higher and technical education, apart from establishment of open educational system and delinking of jobs from degrees, etc. for the first time, Human Resource Development emphasized, regulation of admissions, training, etc. setting-up, autonomous colleges, Research.
1992	National Policy on Education with some Modifications in 1986 Policy and POA, 1992	Based upon National Policy, Educational Policy Education Review Committee (NPERC), and CABE Committee. Some modifications were made in Education Policy, 1986 and POA, 1992.

Source: Goel Aruna and Goel S.L. (2005).

D. Development of Education in Post-Independence Period

The post-independence period of India has been an era of educational expansion; soon after the independence one of the first steps taken up by the Government of India was to convert the Department of Education set up in 1945 to the status of Ministry. It was only after this that the country laid great emphasis on higher education, another important action was taken by the Government of India, by the appointment of the University Education Commission in 1948, under the Chairmanship of a great Educationist, Philosopher Dr. S. Radhakrishnan, the Commission submitted a massive report in three volumes. The report criticized the low educational standards in the Universities, and urged a new education relevant to Indian cultural heritage and to its promising future as an independent state, further it recommended rapid expansion of higher education on priority basis.

On the recommendation of the Commission, in 1953 University Grants Commission was set up but it received statutory status in 1956. Its primary objective was to make grants of money to Universities, later it took responsibilities pertaining to determining, coordinating and maintaining the standards of education in colleges and universities. Seven new universities were created in between 1947-50. The appointment of Education Commission during 1964-66 was the most promising development in education. On the basis of the reports, unprecedented expansion of education facilities at all stages of education including higher education, had taken place.

Further, in the wake of the Report of Education Commission (Kothari Commission), the first National Policy on Education was formulated in 1968. The policy stressed that the educational system must produce young men and women of character and ability committed to national service and development. Only then will education be able to play its vital role in promoting national progress, creating a sense of common citizenship and culture, and strengthening national integration. In the year 1977, the Janata Government came to power and prepared a draft on National Policy on Education (1979). But the very next year the Congress Government came to power again and followed the earlier National Policy on Education of 1968; and the draft policy prepared by Janata Government came to an end.

Making a fresh assessment of status of education in the country, almost a quarter of century later, the National Policy on Education was adopted by Parliament in May, 1986 which reaffirmed that education was a unique investment in the present and the future. The policy urged that in the context of the unprecedented expansion of knowledge, higher education has to become dynamic, constantly covering uncharted and newer areas. The policy recommended for the establishment of 'Open University System' in order to make education more democratic and accessible. It also felt the importance of the Rural Universities to take up the challenges of micro-planning at grassroots for the transformation of the rural areas. It also aimed at providing special access to Colleges and Universities for large sections of society through protective discrimination like reservation of seats in higher education, scholarship and special incentives.

Review of New Education Policy

The National Policy on Education (NPE) envisages a review of the implementation of various parameters of the policy every five years. The Union Government had, in May 1990, appointed a Committee to review NPE, 1986 (NPERC), under the Chairmanship of Acharya Ramamurti. The Committee submitted its report on 26th December,

1990. Three important recommendations of NPERC stated, which have policy implications: (a) Enlarging the scope of Article 45 of the Constitution so as to cover Early Childhood Care and Education (ECCE), (b) Making the right to education a fundamental right and (c) National Council of Higher Education (NCHE): The NPERC did not consider it desirable to set-up a national level superbody to co-ordinate the functioning of various bodies in the field of education like the UGC, ICAR, AICTE, ICME, etc. It felt that two committees—one of the ministers concerned and the other of secretaries—would do.

The most of the recommendations of NPERC were in the area of Programme of Action (POA). Later on, the chairman of the CABE appointed a Committee on 21st July, 1991, to review the implementation of various parameters of NPE taking into consideration the report of the NPERC and other relevant developments; since the policy was formulated and to recommend modifications to be made in NPE. On the bases of the report of NPERC and CABE Committee, some changes were introduced in the National Policy on Education 1986. A new document on Education Policy 1986 with modifications undertaken in 1972 was brought out.

Growth of Universities and Colleges in India

At the time of Independence, only 20 Universities and 500 Colleges were functioning in different parts of the country with an enrolment of around a hundred thousand students. Since then a substantial expansion of higher education institutions[1] is being taken in the country. It can be observed through the data presented in Table 3.2. This implies that government has realized the necessity of higher education for enhancing the quality of human resource and the development of the country.

There has been a considerable increase in the spread of higher educational institutions in the country since 1950-51 to 2009-10; there is around fifteen times increase in universities and about forty-five times boost in colleges during the said period. However, still huge number of higher education institutions are required to expand the coverage; the quantitative expansion is not sufficient condition for imparting higher education; it should simultaneously followed by quality. The Twelfth Five Year Plan has given concurrent attention to quality and its access to all those who desire it in order to achieve the national development goals.

Table 3.2: Growth of Universities/University Level Institutions and Colleges in India, 1950-51 to 2009-10

Year	*Number of Institutions*			*Growth Rate (%)*		
	Universities/ University Level Institutions	*Colleges*	*Total*	*Universities/ University Level Institutions*	*Colleges*	*Total*
1950-51	32	695	727	—	—	—
1960-61	56	1542	1598	5.76	8.30	8.19
1970-71	102	3604	3706	6.18	8.86	8.78
1980-81	133	4722	4855	2.69	2.74	2.74
1990-91	190	7346	7536	3.63	4.52	4.49
2000-01	256	12806	13062	3.03	5.71	5.65
2009-10*	493	31324	31817	7.55	10.45	10.40

Source: 1. UGC, Statistical Abstract, 2003.
2. UGC Annual Reports (Various Issues).
3. *Provisional.

The data presented in Fig. 3.1 indicate that the growth of colleges is much faster than the universities; during sixties and seventies growth rate of higher education institutions were better than remaining period. However, during 2009-10 the growth rate of both universities and colleges are all times high than the before. The trends apprehended that government and various regulating bodies of higher education have adopted liberalized policy[2] for the establishment and functioning of colleges and universities to impart the higher education in the country.

Student Enrolment and Higher Education Institutions

The data presented in Table 3.3 indicate that student enrolment in higher education institutions has substantially increased for the last sixty years. However, the coverage of relevant age-group (18-23) under higher education is very little i.e. about 12 per cent of the relevant age-group of population. Even though there is a significant growth in student enrolment in higher education system, especially in the last two decades, the GER in higher education in India is still about half the world's average GER (24%) and about two-thirds that of the developing countries (18%) and much lower than that of

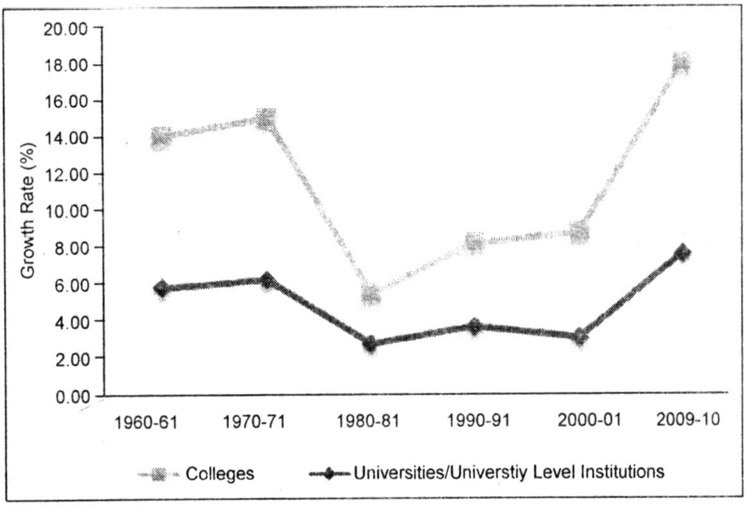

Source: Table 3.2.

Fig. 3.1: Percentage Growth of Universities/University Level Institutions and Colleges in India, 1950-51 to 2009-10

developed nations (58%) (Mid-term Appraisal of the Eleventh Fear Year Plan). It is observed that quantitative expansion of higher education institutions, awareness among public and necessity to have higher degrees are core aspects to increase the enrolment in higher education. The targeted GER in higher education was fixed at 15 per cent by the end of the Eleventh Five Year Plan and was accordingly required to grow by 8.9 per cent annually.

The issue of inclusion of disadvantaged section of the society under higher education segment is required in order to increase the GER in higher education and provide the benefits of higher education; hence a specialized policy need to be implemented to address the issue of inclusion. Similar observations were made by Bhattacharya Joyati (2012) that, inclusion is a very critical issue in India, because of complex disparity in terms of demography, gender, socio-economic parameter and geography. Hence, a uniform policy may not work to ensure inclusion for all; the constraint of each of these groups is to be addressed separately with specific policies and schemes. In this connection, the Twelfth Five Year Plan focused on inclusiveness.

As observed (Fig. 3.2) during sixties and seventies both higher education institutions and student enrolment growth rate was higher and growth of enrolment was all times high during 1970-71; which

Table 3.3: Growth of Higher Education Institutions and Enrolment in India, 1950-51 to 2009-10

Year	*Total of Institutions*	*Student Enrolment*	*Growth Rate (%)*	
			Total Institutions	Total Enrolment
1950-51	727	173696	—	—
1960-61	1598	556559	8.19	12.35
1970-71	3706	1953700	8.78	13.38
1980-81	4855	2752437	2.74	3.49
1990-91	7536	4924886	4.49	5.99
2000-01	13062	8399443	5.65	5.48
2009-10*	31817	14624990	10.40	5.70

Source: (1) UGC, Statistical Abstract, 2003.
(2) UGC Annual Reports (Various Issues).
(3) *Provisional.

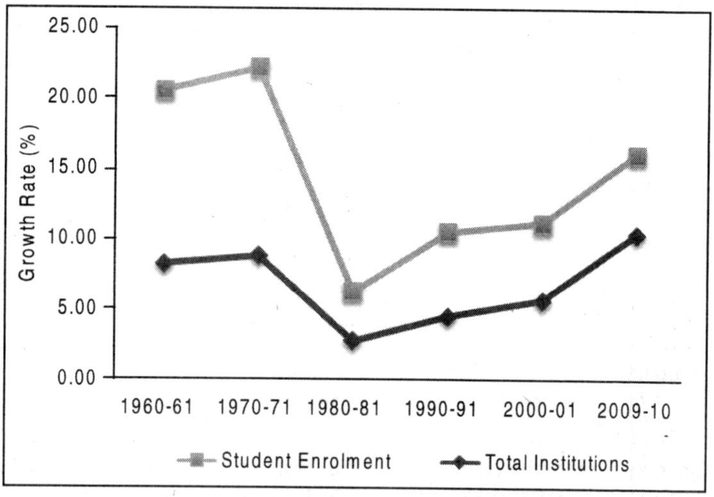

Source: Table 3.3.

Fig. 3.2: Percentage Growth of Higher Education Institutions and Enrolment in India, 1950-51 to 2009-10

is much higher in entire decades; also much higher than education institutions. Later on growth of enrolment is slow downed. During 2009-10, the growth of higher education institutions is all times high for entire period. It is observed that both the institutions and enrolment are not growing at uniform rate.

Number of Teachers for Higher Education in India

The data presented in Table 3.4 shows that teachers and students at higher education institutions are increasing considerably since 1950-51 to 2009-10. However, the growth of students is much faster than teachers in entire decades except 1980-81. The huge gap between the growth of students and teachers would lead to poor Student-Teacher Ratio (STR) at higher education level. The STR is an important factor to determine the quality of education. Sharma Sheetal (2006) estimated in his study that, during 1995-96 the teacher student ratio was 1:19.14 and it is increasing year after year; it registered at 1:21.15 in the year 2002-03.

Many research studies found that, the young talent with necessary qualification to teach in higher education institutions are increasing in the country. This enormous reservoir of educated young talent with potential to teach needs to be tapped to meet quality in higher education; the government should recruit more teachers and fill-up the all vacant posts to attain ideal STR at higher education level.

Table 3.4: Number of Students and Teachers in Higher Education Institutions in India, 1950-51 to 2010-11

Year	*Number of Students*	*Number of Teachers*	*Growth Rate (%)*	
			Students	*Teachers*
1950-51	173696	23549	—	—
1960-61	556559	59673	12.35	9.74
1970-71	1953700	128876	13.38	8.00
1980-81	2752437	193341	3.49	4.14
1990-91	4924886	263125	5.99	3.13
2000-01	8399443	411628	5.48	4.58
2010-11	16975390	816966	7.29	7.10

Source: 1. MHRD for 1950-51 & 1960-61 and UGC for 1970-71 onwards.
2. *Provisional.

The issue of quality is another area of concern; until now, there is no efficient mechanism to assess quality in our education system. Governments are making efforts to improve quality in higher education; but implementation part is in hands of teachers of all levels of education system. The role of teachers is significant in two terms firstly, continuous upgradation of his/her knowledge and secondly, provide education to the students in innovative manner (Trivedi,

2010). If the teachers perform their duty as mentioned above the quality in education would be easily realized. Similar observation is made by Bhattacharya Joyati (2012) that, in higher education the quality depends on the quality of students and the teachers and their commitment to excel. In view of the shortage of quality teachers and students, creation of a very competitive higher education set up and world class universities would remain an arduous task for our government.

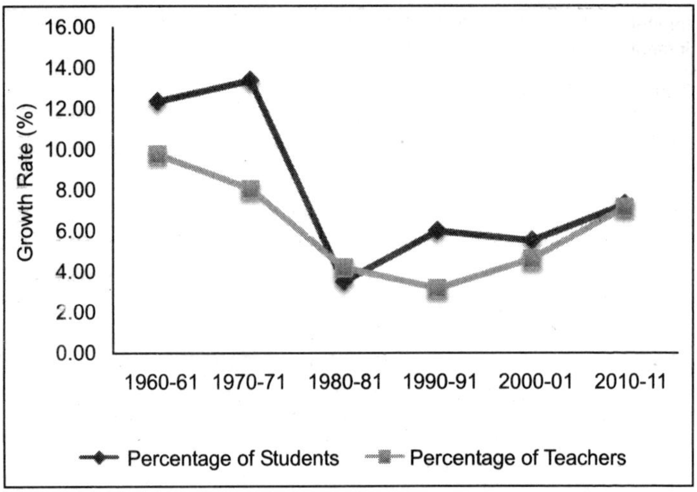

Source: Table 3.4.

Fig. 3.3: Percentage Growth of Students and Teachers in Higher Education Institutions in India, 1950-51 to 2010-11

Types of Universities/Institutions Imparting Higher Education in India

In India various types of higher education institutions are imparting education in the country; the data presented in Table 3.5 indicate that, State Universities contributing immensely to higher education in the country; they are at first position; followed by Deemed-to-be Universities[3] are declared by the Government of India as per section of the UGC Act, 1956. As a result of liberalization policy of the governments in recent years State Private Universities are increasing in the country and these are in third place. It is predicted that in future the number of Deemed-to-be-Universities and State Private Universities are going to increase in the country.

Table 3.5: Type of Universities/University Level Institutions in India during 2010

Type of Institutions	*Number*	*Percentage*
Central Universities	42	8.52
State Universities	256	51.93
State Private Universities	60	12.17
Institutions established under State Legislative	5	1.01
Institutions Deemed to be Universities	130	26.37
Institutions of National Importance	--	--
Total	493	100

Source: UGC Annual Report 2009-10

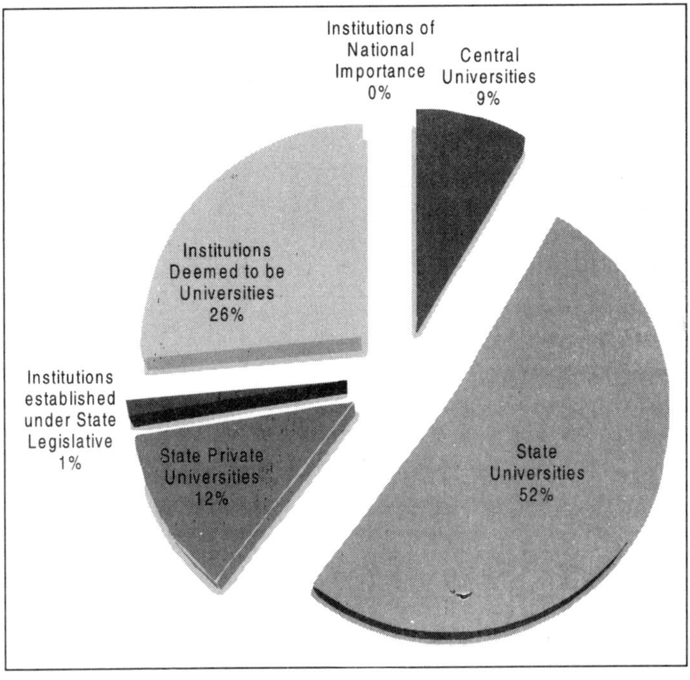

Source: Table 3.5.

Fig. 3.4: Percentage-wise Type of Universities/University Level Institutions in India during 2010

Growth of Women Colleges in India

Women constitute almost half of the total population; but colleges established exclusively for women are very insignificant in the country. The data presented in Table 3.6 indicate that, very small numbers of women colleges are functioning in the country; around 1/10 portion of women colleges are imparting education.

Table 3.6: Growth of Women Colleges in India, 1950-51 to 2009-10

Year	*Total Number of Colleges*	*Total Number of Women Colleges*	*Percentage of Women Colleges*
1950-51	695	77	11.08
1960-61	1542	169	10.96
1970-71	3604	426	11.82
1980-81	4722	609	12.90
1990-91	7346	874	11.90
2000-01	12806	1578	12.32
2009-10*	31324	3432	10.96

Source: Various UGC Annual Reports.
*Provisional.

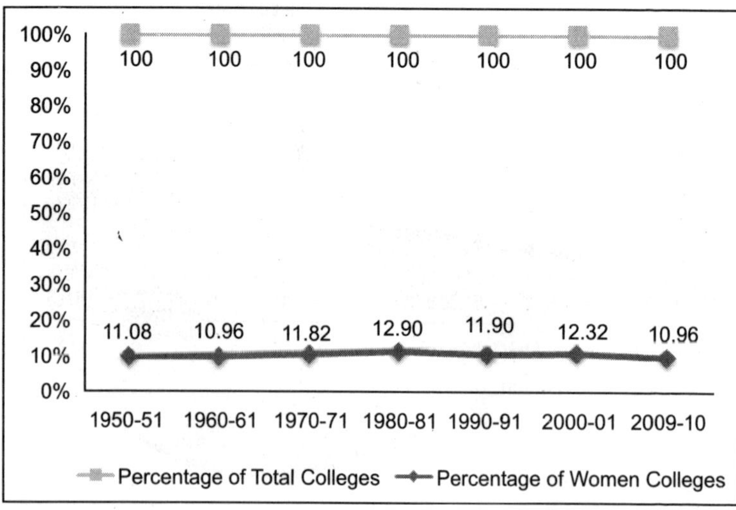

Source: Table 3.6.

Fig. 3.5: Percentage of Growth of Women Colleges in India

There was negligible fluctuation in the growth of women colleges from 1950-51 to 2009-10; hence the decadal growth of women colleges remained almost same. However, an important observation can be drawn i.e. during 1980-81 and 2000-01 marginal percentage of increase was registered in women colleges (see Fig. 3.5); it may be because of the 1986 National Policy on Education provided special support services for women education and removed the hindrances in spreading of women education; and the 'Programme of Action, 1992' also positively contributed for increase in percentage of women colleges, enrolment and their status in the nation; ultimately the main purpose behind the establishment of women colleges are to expand the coverage of women under higher education and to empower the women through providing education facilities.

Sex-wise Enrolment in Higher Education

The data presented in Table 3.7 indicate that, the enrolment of women is increasing slowly from 1950-51 to 2009-10; however, a significant growth was registered during 2000-01 i.e. about 10 per cent.

Table 3.7: Women Enrolment in Higher Education in India, 1950-51 to 2009-10

Year	*Male Enrolment*	*Female Enrolment*	*Total Enrolment*	*Percentage of Male*	*Percentage of Female*
1950-51	156326	17370	173696	90.00	10.00
1960-61	467510	89049	556559	84.00	16.00
1970-71	1521932	431768	1953700	77.90	22.10
1980-81	2003774	748663	2752437	72.80	27.20
1990-91	3486819	1438067	4924886	70.80	29.20
2000-01	5090062	3309381	8399443	60.60	39.40
2009-10*	8544617	6080373	14624990	58.42	41.58

Source: 1. Various UGC Annual Reports.

2. *Provisional.

Even though, the women enrolment and her position in higher education is improving; it is not a satisfactory achievement; because still large percentage of women belongs to relevant age group (18-23) are deprived of higher education opportunities in the country. The Parliamentary Standing Committee on HRD (2006) expressed that "it is not a realistic way of projecting the position of women in the higher education. These figures become meaningless if compared with the proportion of women in the age group of 18 to 23 years to the total population in this group. Secondly, their participation (40 per cent) in higher education becomes abysmally low because this percentage is, in fact, of the 7 per cent of the total youth in the eligible age group that is currently in higher education." It clearly indicates that their participation in higher education is quite disappointing, so it is necessary to provide more facilities to increase women participation in higher education, which will contribute for development of the country.

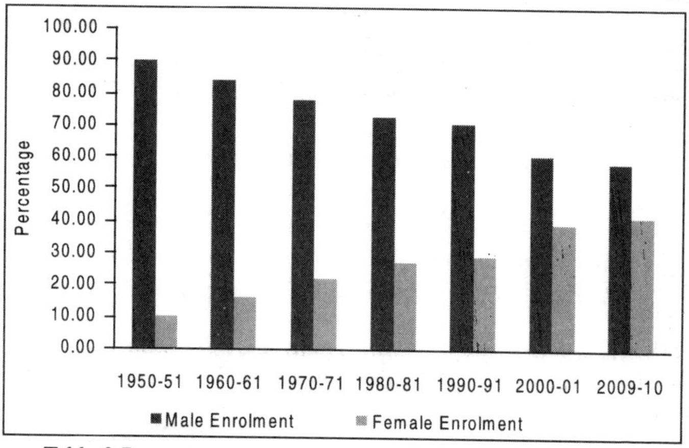

Source: Table 3.7.

Fig. 3.6: Comparison of Male and Female Enrolment in Higher Education in India, 1950-51 to 2009-10

Faculty-wise Women Enrolment

The data presented in Table 3.8 indicate that, majority of women have opted Arts and Humanities discipline for higher studies; followed by Science courses, Commerce/Management and Engineering/ Technology and Medicine courses respectively. However, it is a matter of great concern that, women enrolment is very small for Management, Engineering/Technology, Medicine, even though these fields are in great demand.

Research Degrees Awarded in the Country

The data presented in Table 3.9 indicate that, during all the referred

Table 3.8: Women Enrolment by Faculty: 2009-10

Faculty	*Women Enrolment*	*Percentage of Women Enrolment*
Arts	2776289	45.66
Science	1214864	19.98
Commerce/Management	967392	15.91
Education	224974	3.7
Engineering/Technology	467581	7.69
Medicine	234702	3.86
Agriculture	16417	0.27
Veterinary Science	4256	0.07
Law	84517	1.39
Others	89381	1.47
Total	6080373	100

Source: UGC Annual Report: 2009-10.
*Provisional.

periods, majority of doctoral degrees awarded belong to Arts and Science subjects. These two faculties together accounted for 66 per cent of the total number of doctoral degrees awarded in 2008-09. Science faculty positioned at first place with highest number of doctoral degrees in the beginning three decades i.e. from 1961-62 to 1981-82, later it positioned at second place during 1991-92 and 2000-01; again Science faculties retained their first position during 2008-09.

Table 3.9: Doctoral Degrees Awarded in India, 1961-62 to 2008-09

Subjects	*1961-62*	*1970-71*	*1981-82*	*1991-92*	*2000-01*	*2008-09**
Arts	314	876	2347	3489	4398	3496
Science	401	1103	2846	3226	3727	3603
Comm. & Management	15	58	173	409	621	724
Education	9	42	178	254	399	403
Engg. & Tech.	20	99	190	299	778	1141
Medical	14	33	66	107	221	298
Agricultural	41	216	471	653	889	427
Vet. Science	NA	26	93	129	110	93
Law	1	5	14	60	105	152
Others	NA	3	26	117	296	396
Total	815	2461	6404	8743	11534	10781
Growth Rate (%)	—	13.07	10.04	3.16	3.13	-0.84

Note: NA: Not Available.
Source: Various UGC Annual Reports.
*Provisional.

It is noted that, the number of the doctoral degree holders in the faculty of commerce did not rise high during first 20 years, later on commerce became more popular. In case of Engineering and Technology, Medicine and Agriculture fields doctoral degrees awarded are increasing in recent decades, but it is not enough to meet the growing demand; since, faculty of these areas have ample demand and required in the country as well as in the world.

On the other hand, the growth of doctoral degrees awarded in the country is higher during 1970-71 and 1980-81; later the growth was slowed down and on 2008-09 a negative growth registered on doctoral degrees awarded in entire periods. However, the quality of doctoral degrees and their contribution to the nation is the matter of concern. The choice of subjects for Ph.Ds and quality of academic research leading to them are both considerably poor in India. Any subject, however trivial, is good enough for Ph.D. A mere possession of a Ph.D. does not guarantee any significant value addition in Indian conditions (Gupta, Pradeep, 2011).

Expenditure on Education under Five Year Plans

The data presented in Table 3.10 provides an analysis of plan expenditure on education during Five Year Plan periods; trends indicate that elementary education received highest portion of the education plan outlay in all FYPs; and except Fourth and Fifth Five Year Plans higher education was in third position receiving small amount of finance. Under First Five Year Plan just 9 per cent of total expenditure was made to higher education, proceeding plans it increased, the Fifth Five Year Plan received all times highest share, after that the percentage share of higher education expenditure is decreasing continuously. Elementary education received the least priority during the Fourth and Sixth plan period and it has now begun to receive the highest priority in plan expenditure. It is observed that quantum of plan allocation for higher education is depending on the decision regarding the quantum of plan allocation for elementary education.

The trends in Fig. 3.7 indicate that Fifth Five Year Plan onwards government started reducing its financial support for higher education; after 1990 plan expenditure is declining steeply; it has been found that a severe cut in Central planned resources for Higher Education in the Tenth Plan. At the same time, government has given more

Table 3.10: Expenditure on Education under Five Year Plans

Five Year Plans	*Elementary (%)*	*Secondary (%)*	*Higher (%)*	*Total Expenditure (in lakh)*
I	56	13	9	15,300
II	35	19	18	27,300
III	34	18	15	58,900
IV	30	18	25	78,600
V	33	13	28	91,200
VI	30	25	18	2,04,000
VII	34	22	14	8,50,000
VIII	47	18	12.4	8,52,190
IX	65.7	10.5	10.0	24,90,850
X	78	6	7	59,122.65

Source: Five Year Plans, Annual Plans and MHRD Reports.

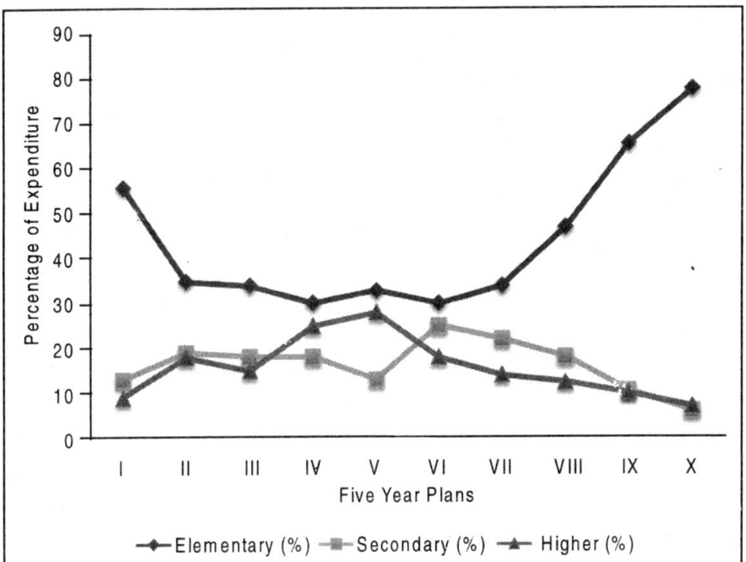

Source: Table 3.10.

Fig. 3.7: Percentage of Expenditure on Different Levels of Education under Five Year Plans

importance to elementary education; consequently the share of elementary education under the Ninth and Tenth Five Year Plan was increased significantly. It has been suggested that higher education institutions should start to generate the financial sources by increasing fees and undertaking research and consultancy activities.

Public spending on higher education is justified on the grounds that it generates positive externalities since it is a merit good. Equally, there is an argument that public spending on higher education should be discouraged since private benefits far outweigh social benefits. Consequently, public subsidization of higher education benefits the rich, particularly in elite higher education systems in India (Tilak, 2005). However, there are convincing arguments on both sides, the Government has accepted higher education as a merit good and continues to found it. However, the financial situation of higher education is worried and in need of a quick solution.

Conclusion

The foregoing analysis reveals that in Ancient period number of intellectual learned scholars such as Faheeyan, Hiuen Tsang, Alberuni, Megasthenes and host of others visited to this noble land from different corners of the world to enrich their knowledge and fulfil their thirst for knowledge; on the other hand, number of foreign students were studying in our ancient universities viz. Nalanda, Valabhi and Vikramshila renowned as international centres of learning. It evidences that, India has the rich inheritance, magnetic qualities and profundity of knowledge from the dawn of civilization.

A phenomenal growth in number of higher education institutions/ universities has taken place; but the quantitative expansion is not accompanied with qualitative one is a matter of serious concern. The growth of students is much faster than teachers in entire decades; but during 1990-91 growth rate of teachers was registered much declining. The huge difference between the growth of students and teachers would lead to poor Student-Teacher Ratio (STR) at higher education level. State Universities contributing immensely to higher education in the country; it is predicted that in future the number of Deemed-to-be-Universities and State Private Universities are going to increase in the country. On the other hand, due to the inadequate provision of budgetary resources; the Indian higher education institutions/ universities are facing financial difficulties; in this case, the present budgetary allocation to higher education should be increased and higher education institutions/universities have to generate resources through internal sources.

Notes

1. During 21st Century government initiated much liberalization policy for expansion of higher education by autonomous colleges, permanently unaided colleges, deemed university status and institutions of national importance, opening up of private and foreign institutions, distance education centres, courses etc.
2. The Central Government establishes Central Universities and it is also responsible for declaration of Educational Institutions as 'Deemed-to-be-University' on the recommendation of the UGC. Deemed-to-be-Universities are institutions that are conferred the status of a University by virtue of their long tradition of teaching, or specialization and excellence in a particular area of knowledge. Institutions of national importance are established through Acts of Parliament and these are empowered to award their own degrees e.g. IITs. State Governments are responsible for establishment of State Universities and Colleges.

4

World Trade Organization and General Agreement on Trade in Services

An Overview

Introduction

This chapter provides a clear and concise explanation about the World Trade Organization (WTO) and General Agreement on Trade in Service (GATS). This basic information facilitates to understand the framework of WTO and GATS, further it becomes easy to know the implications of GATS agreements on higher education services.

Origin of General Agreement on Tariffs and Trade (GATT)

The 1930s worldwide depression and Second World War, both badly affected the world trade, many countries got down together to work on ways and means to promote international trade. This led to conduct of negotiations in 1947 among 23 countries at Geneva and they signed an agreement related to remove/reduce the protectionism policies and to revive the economies from the recession. This agreement became known as General Agreement on Tariffs and Trade (GATT), came into force from January 1, 1948.

Objectives of GATT

The objectives of the GATT were as follows:

- To ensure a better living standard amongst the member countries,

- To increase the effective demand for real income growth and goods,
- To develop the full use of the resources of the world,
- To minimize tariffs for expanding production and international trade, and
- To provide equal opportunities to all countries in international market for trading purpose without any favour.

There were 8 rounds of negotiations held among member countries between 1947 and the last year of GATT i.e. 1994. The feature of the negotiations in all the rounds during 1947 to 1960 was tariffs. The negotiation in other rounds included anti-dumping measures etc. The 8th round was entirely different from the previous rounds because it included a number of new issues for consideration; which became known as the Uruguay Round.

Uruguay Round and Dunkel Proposals

The 8th round of GATT popularly known as Uruguay Round was started in September, 1986. Mr. Arthur Dunkel, the then Director General of GATT compiled a very detailed document, popularly known as Dunkel Proposal and submitted it on 20th December, 1991, which envisages trade liberalizations in many areas like Trade Related Investment Measures (TRIMs), Trade Related Intellectual Property Rights (TRIPs), Other Services, Textiles, Clothing and Agriculture Subsidies. The 8th round of negotiation covers a wide range of subjects like subsidies, safeguards, Market Access, TRIPs, TRIMs and trade in services. An agreement regarding multilateral trading system was finally signed by 124 countries and India is also one of them signing it in Muarrakesh, Morocco, on 15th April, 1994.

Establishment of World Trade Organization (WTO)

The signing of the Final Act of the Uruguay Round by member nations of GATT in April 1994 paved the way for the setting up of the World Trade Organisation (WTO). An agreement to this effect was signed by 124 members. The WTO Agreement came into force on January 1, 1995 and India became a founder member of the World Trade Organisation, by ratifying the WTO Agreement on December 30,

1994. The WTO is a new international organization set up as a permanent body and is designed to play the role of a watchdog in the spheres of trade in goods, trade in services, foreign investment, intellectual property rights etc.

It is officially defined as "the legal and institutional foundation of the multilateral trading system". Unlike the GATT, WTO is a permanent organization created by international treaty ratified by the governments and legislatures of member states. The WTO has global status like that of the International Monetary Fund (IMF) and the World Bank (IBRD). It being a prime international body offers multilateral trade negotiations to members and resolves the trade disputes and problems of member states.

Administration

Director General is the highest official of the organization to look after day to day working. General Council of WTO elects Director General for the period of 4 years. The present Director General of WTO is Mr. Pascal Lamy, who is assisted by four deputies from different member states. The WTO's ruling apex body is the General Council, which includes each member country's permanent representatives. It meets in Geneva on an average of once a month. Its supreme authority of policy making is the Ministerial Conference, which held once in every two years.

Membership

According to the WTO Report (WTR-2003), at the end of April 2003, 146 countries were the members of WTO. Hong Kong, China, Taiwan, Mangolia and Macao are among the new members of WTO. But in Hong Kong Conference, held in Hong Kong on 10-14th September, 2006, 2 more nations also got the membership of WTO; as on June 2012 the membership of WTO is increased to 155. Vietnam is the last member and there are presently 30 countries in the process of accession to the WTO.

Objectives of WTO

The WTO has following objectives viz.:

- To improve standard of living of people in the member countries.
- To enlarge production and trade of goods and services.
- To ensure optimum utilization of world resources and to protect environment.
- To accept the concept of sustainable development.
- To ensure full employment and extensive increase in effective demand.

Features of WTO

The unique features of WTO are:

- Unlike the GATT, WTO is a legal entity and a huge organizational body with a large secretariat.
- The WTO is not an agent of the United Nations, like the International Monetary Fund (IMF) and the World Bank (WB).
- All the WTO members have equal rights, but the IMF and the World Bank have weighted voting facility.
- Unlike the GATT, the agreements under the WTO are permanent and binding to the member countries.
- The WTO has a Dispute Settlement Mechanism; which is quicker and binding on the members, but the GATT hadn't such facility.
- Unlike the GATT, the WTO's approach is rule-based and time-bound.
- Unlike the GATT, the WTO has a wider coverage, viz. trade in goods as well as services.
- Unlike the GATT, the WTO has a focus on Trade-Related Aspects of Intellectual Property Rights and several other issues of agreements.

Functions of WTO

The broad functions of WTO are as follows:

- To facilitate the implementation, administration and operation of Multilateral and Plurilateral Trade Agreements of the international trade.

- To provide a platform to member countries to negotiate related to multilateral trade relations.
- To administer the Rules and Procedure connected to Dispute settlement.
- To administer and implement rules and provisions related to the Trade Policy Review Mechanism (TPRM).
- To co-operate with the International Monetary Fund (IMF), The International Bank for Reconstruction and Development (IBRD) and its affiliated agencies for establishing coherence in universal economic policy determination.

Organizational Structure of the WTO

The Organizational structure of the WTO is intended based on three hierarchical levels. The hierarchies from the top to bottom are shown in chart 4.1.

Ministerial Conference

The Ministerial Conference is the policy and strategy making body; and it composed of representatives of all the member countries of WTO. Ministerial Conference shall have the authority to take decision on all matters relating to multilateral trade agreements. Further, the Ministerial Conference shall carry out the functions of the WTO and take necessary actions to this effect.

General Council

There shall be a General Council composed of representatives of all the members, which shall meet as number of times as appropriate. In the intervals between meetings of the Ministerial Conference, its functions shall be conducted by the General Council. The General Council shall also carry out the functions assigned to it by this Agreement. The General Council has other wings called Bodies—like Dispute Settlement Body and Trade Policy Review Body.

- Dispute Settlement Body (DSB) is the one where it can set up panels to make decisions on disputes between members.
- Trade Policy Review Body (TPRB) oversees the reviews of member countries' trade policies as described in the Trade Policy Review Mechanism (TPRM).

Chart 4.1
Organizational Structure of WTO

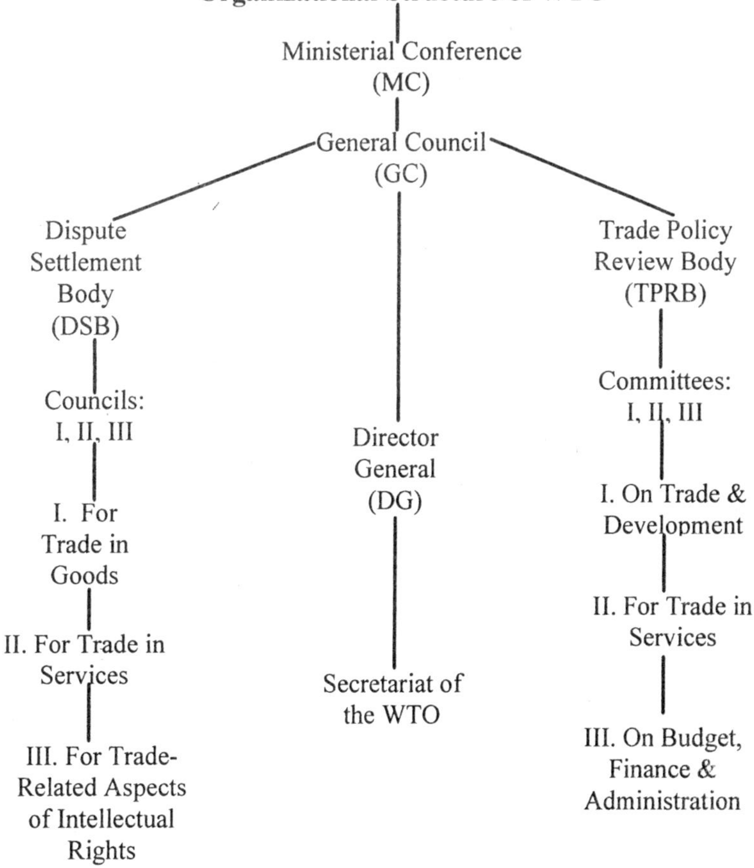

Multitude of Councils, Committees and Bodies

Councils

The third level in the hierarchy is Councils. There are three councils, viz.:

- ***Council for Trade in Goods***: It manages the implementation and functioning of all agreements relating to trade in goods.

- ***Council for Trade in Services***: It oversees the implementation of all the agreements relating to trade in services.
- ***Council for Trade Related Aspects of Intellectual Property Rights (TRAIPS)***: This supervises the implementations and functioning of all the agreements relating to this area.

Committees and Bodies

The General Council delegates powers, responsibilities and authorities to these bodies.

Committees

There are also a number of committees that are intended to monitor certain aspects of the trading system and provide recommendations. Ministerial Conference constituted three committees, viz.:

- ***Committee on Trade and Development***: This Committee is concerned with the issues pertaining to developing countries and particularly with least developed countries.
- ***Committee on Balance of Payments***: Some WTO member countries resort to trade restrictive measures with a view to cope with their balance of payments problems. The Committee on Balance of Payments arranges consultations among such countries.
- ***Committee on Budget, Finance and Administration***: This Committee deals with the issues relating to the budget, finance and administration of WTO.

Bodies

Plurilateral agreements of the WTO have their management bodies. These management bodies report to the General Council. Some of the plurilateral agreements having management bodies include: civil aircraft, government procurement, dairy products, bovine meat etc.

Dispute Settlement Mechanism of WTO

The rapid growth of foreign trade leads competition among the countries globally. This competition, in turn, made the countries to adopt win-lose strategies in the foreign trade, which in turn, created disputes between the countries. WTO has facilitated member countries by providing Dispute Settlement Body for solving their trade disputes. In recent years, developing countries are emerged as active partners in the global trade and trade disputes are increased among developed and developing countries.

The Dispute Settlement Body (DSB) has the sole authority to establish dispute settlement panels, adopt panel and appellate reports, maintain supervision of implementation of rulings and recommendations and authorize suspension of concession in the eve of non-implementation of recommendation. The proper functioning of DSB is need of the hour, as it contributes to the strengthening and consolidation of the WTO and the multilateral trading system.

WTO, in one of its recent reports observed that multilateral dispute mechanism is used more frequently by the developing countries than the advanced countries. The phenomenon is more prominent in WTO compared to that in GATT. Dispute Settlement Body established two panels on 5th March, 1996, at the request of Philippines and Costa Rica. Out of the four active dispute settlement panels, three of them are involved in the settlement of disputes of the developing countries.

WTO: A Multilateral Forum

The International Monetary Fund (IMF) and the International Bank for Reconstruction and Development (IBRD) are most important and influencing international bodies in the world. On the other hand, the WTO has been observed as the third pillar of the global business which is the only multilateral forum to discuss trade liberalization and settle disputes. The WTO has added new dynamism to the international business environment through the reduction of duties, tariffs, non-tariff barriers like quotas and controls. Finally, the WTO has enlarged the market access opportunities and provided efficient rules for undistorted competition among the world countries.

Ministerial Conference of the WTO

The Ministerial Conference is the policy and strategy making Supreme Body; and it composed of representatives of all the member countries of WTO. Ministerial Conference shall have the authority to take decision on all matters relating to multilateral trade agreements. Further, the Ministerial Conference shall carry out the functions of the WTO and take actions necessary to this effect.

First Ministerial Conference of the WTO

The First Ministerial Conference of WTO was held in Singapore on 9th-13th December, 1996. Totally 128 member countries attended the meeting. Among the conclusions, of major conclusion of the Conference was the establishment of three working groups, respectively, on trade and investment, trade and competition policy, and transparency in government procurement, plus a mandate to conduct a study on trade facilitation.

The Conference rejected the use of labour standards for projectionists' purpose; comparative advantage of low wage developing countries must in no way be put into question. The members took a decision to organize a meeting with the United Nations Conference on Trade and Development (UNCTAD), aid agencies and other organizations to help the least developed countries. A decision was taken to set up two Working Groups, one for examining the relationship between trade and investment was taken. It would study the issues by members relating to the interaction between trade and competition policy; another group for conducting a study on transparency in Government procurement practices; taking account of the national policies. Other highlights of the meet were; negotiations on basic telecommunications were to be completed by February, 1997; reaffirmation to the work of the International Labour Organization and commitment to the observance of internationally recognized core labour standards.

Second Ministerial Conference of WTO

The Second Ministerial Conference of the WTO was held on May 18th to 20th, 1998 at Geneva. The two important decisions were taken; viz.: (i) a decision to establish a mechanism to ensure full and faithful implementation of existing multilateral agreements, and (ii) rejection of projectionist measures and accepting for open and transparent rule based trading system.

This meeting of the WTO stated that ministerial meeting decisions are crucial for multilateral trading system and for expanding global trade, creating more jobs and raising the living standards of the people in the entire world. It also stated that the benefits of multilateral trading system must flow to the developing needs of the third World Countries.

Third Ministerial Conference of WTO

The Third Ministerial Conference of the WTO comprising of 137 members was held on November 30th to December 3rd, 1999 at Seattle (USA). This meeting was a failure as the developing nations jointly protested against the lack of transparency and imposition of the views of the rich on the poor countries in the negotiations.

The two important reasons were responsible for failure of the Seattle round talks; firstly, American determination on inclusion of labour standards. For this, developing countries opposed, they felt that the talks about labour standards as a play to prevent their products form entering the western countries. Secondly, reluctance of European Union to liberalise agriculture. The EU was unwilling to reduce its heavy export subsidy to farmers. Unless the developed world cuts down its export subsidy significantly, developing countries will not gain from the global agricultural trade. Among the various issues discussed in the conference following two important issues came under limelight, viz.:

- *Trade and Environment* — The EU idea to "mainstream" environment and the US proposal that members have the right to set high environmental standards unaffected by trade rules were opposed by some developing countries, including India. However, there was a good degree of support for the US - Cairns Group proposal for removal of environmentally damaging subsidies. The TRIPS-CBD convergence for conserving biodiversity and traditional knowledge sought by India and the developing countries were supported by some.
- *Investment and Competition Policy* — The EC proposal to launch negotiations immediately was opposed. Most developing countries were in favour of continuation of the work programme in the WTO to prepare for negotiations to be started in the Fourth Ministerial Conference. India, Malaysia, HK China and Pakistan were in favour of open-ended continuation of the study process commenced at Singapore.

Fourth Ministerial Conference of WTO

The Fourth Ministerial Conference of WTO was held at Doha (Qatar) from 9th-14th November, 2001. The Fourth WTO Ministerial Conference reaffirmed the governments' commitment to the objectives of sustainable development. The outcome, termed The Doha 'Development' Agenda, came in the form of a Ministerial Declaration and a Decision on Implementation-related Issues and Concerns. The Declaration defines areas for collective study and negotiation and establishes a negotiating infrastructure and terms. The mandate to engage on a variety of issue-areas include the WTO's 'built-in agenda', (mainly, agricultural policy reform and further liberalization of trade in services), as well as negotiations on industrial tariffs; anti-dumping and subsidies; rules on regional trade agreements; dispute settlement; and environment and fisheries subsidies. The Declaration also sets the ground for talks and possible future negotiations on the so-called 'Singapore' issues – investment; competition policy; transparency in government procurement; and trade facilitation – despite strong opposition by many developing countries to expand the WTO's agenda to these 'new' areas. In this connection, India underlined the need for resolving the implementation issues arising from the current agreements in a time bound manner before addressing new issues for negotiations.

The substantial outcome of the Doha Ministerial Conference is the work programme aimed at reduction in custom's tariffs and opening up of agriculture and services. Exporters of farm goods can expect to benefit from the reduction of domestic support and export subsidies in Europe and the U.S.

In this Conference the decision on the Agreement on Trade-Related Intellectual Property Rights (TRIPS) and Public Health was a victory for underdeveloped countries, with this India made significant gains on public health concerns in the TRIPS agreement. The agreement over amendment to TRIPS, which would allow countries access to low price patented drugs in case of a public health emergency, was a victory for India. The lead up to Doha witnessed the strengthening of developing country capacities to establish coalitions and present their concerns in a coordinated manner. The rise in influence of developing countries is reflected in the development focus of the new round (the 'Doha Development' Agenda) and the increased emphasis on integrating developing countries into the WTO system through greater capacity building, technical assistance and special and differential treatment. This renewed focus on developing country members will impact on the future work programme of the WTO and the resources allocated to their involvement.

Fifth Ministerial Conference of WTO

The Fifth Ministerial Conference of WTO was held at Cancun (Mexico) from 10th-14th September, 2003. Cancun Conference aimed at revival of talks, which already started at Doha in 2001 and to be concluded by the end of 2004, on opening up of trade to encourage growth in the world economy. The Cancun Ministerial Conference was meant mainly to be a forum to review the progress of negotiations under the Doha Work Programme mandated at Doha and give guidance/directions wherever necessary with the decision expected only on one outstanding issue namely, the status of the Singapore issues.

In this Conference, disagreements were raised viz. disagreement regarding imbalance in agriculture trade, market access improvements of industrial goods, disagreement on Draft Ministerial Text proposed on September 14, 2003 and unsatisfaction of developing countries towards the agriculture (farm subsidies), for these reasons, Cancun talks remained failure.

The important positive outcomes of Cancun Meet were the solidarity expressed by developing countries for protecting their interests and their ability to stay together, further the formation of G-20 by the developing countries, which is protecting the interest of developing member nations.

Sixth Ministerial Conference of WTO

The Sixth Ministerial Conference of WTO was held at Hong Kong on December 13th to 18th, 2005. Under this Conference developing countries were benefited certain extent that, particularly, in respect of agriculture, India has gained in that the deal not only ensures that there would be no restraint on the Government's ability to provide domestic support, it also permits the developing nations to protect farmers against unfair competition from imports. The phasing out of export subsidies on agricultural products by 2013 is claimed to be the biggest single concession wrested from the developed countries.

Even the deal on cotton, expected to benefit some of the poorer African countries, is subject to an agreement being reached on eliminating all export subsidies by the end of 2006. Under this arrangement, while the US will abolish export subsidies on cotton this year, India and other developing countries can retain higher tariffs to protect their farmers and ensure that food and livelihood concerns are met. Their need for a special safeguard mechanism based on price and volume trigger has been recognised.

In Non-Agriculture Market Access (NAMA), developing countries are not required to cut tariffs to the same extent as the developed countries. While the principle of 'less than full reciprocity' has been recognised, there is no agreement on the exact mechanics for such reductions. Only subsequent discussions will bear out whether the developing countries have given away too much under NAMA in return for concessions in agriculture.

The EU finally agreed to do away export subsidies on agricultural products by 2013 thereby contributing to the most visible result. India and Brazil, two large countries deeply involved in agricultural issues, led the discussions on behalf of all developing countries. The smaller developing countries actually showed tremendous resistance and alliance-building efforts during the negotiations.

Introduction of GATS

In 1995, during the Uruguay round, the GATT was replaced by the World Trade Organization (WTO). At that time, a decision was made to broaden the talks to include trade in services and expand participation. That was done under the umbrella of the WTO through the General Agreement on Trade in Services (GATS), set up as the framework for negotiations about trade in services. GATS is a voluntary and multilateral agreement based upon the premise that progressive liberalization of trade in commercial services will promote economic growth in WTO member-countries. It provides legally enforceable right to grade in all services and covers all services except those provided entirely by government. GATS has two components: (1) The Framework Agreement containing 29 Articles, and (2) A number of Annexes, Ministerial Decisions, Schedules of Commitment etc. The agreement presently covers 12 specified services, viz. (i) Business Services; (ii) Communication Services; (iii) Construction and Engineering Services; (iv) Distribution Services; (v) Education Services; (vi) Environment Services; (vii) Financial Services; (viii) Health Services; (ix) Tourism and Travel Services; (x) Recreation, Culture and Sporting Services; finally (xi) Other Services which not elsewhere classified.

Once a nation becomes a member of GATS, it is subject to the general obligations of GATS and makes specific commitments regarding Market Access and National Treatment in specific sectors (such as education). There are costs for not signing GATS; a country outside the agreement risks not having equal access to those markets and losing favourable or unfettered access to markets in critical export areas. At present, 47 member nations have agreed to include at least one sector of education under GATS.

Aims of GATS

The goals are to expand free trade in services, open markets, and facilitate to achieve economic growth for all countries. The goals for higher education as a service include removing restrictions on market access and barriers to competition in higher education.

Modes of Trade in Services

Modes of supply means services can be traded in four ways, these four modes apply to all service sectors in GATS. It is necessary to understand what kind of education services will be covered by GATS. In this connection, Table 4.1 provides the meaning of each mode and illustrates the four modes of supply under education services.

The Important Commitments of GATS

There is a hierarchy of obligations with general obligations applying to all members, followed by specific commitments specified by each member. National commitments serve as the basis for negotiations between member countries that are signatories to GATS. The two levels of commitment are:

- **General obligations** (e.g., Most Favoured Nations Treatment and Transparency). These obligations apply to all services. For example, Most Favoured Nations Treatment requires that members extend equal treatment to each other's service suppliers. Thus, GATS members are entitled to conditions of access equal to the most favourable treatment given to any other nation.
- **Specific commitments.** These refer to member country's commitments to Market Access and National Treatment for specific sectors (such as education). Each government

Table 4.1: Mode of Supply

Mode of Supply According to GATS	*Explanation*	*Examples in Higher Education*	*Size/Potential of market*
1. Cross Border Supply	The provision of a service where the service crosses the border (excludes the physical movement of the consumer).	-distance education -e-learning -virtual universities	-currently a relatively small market -seen to have great potential through the use of new Information Communication Technology (ICTs) and especially the Internet, but difficult to monitor quality.
2. Consumption Abroad	The provision of the service where the consumer to the country of the supplier.	-students who go to another country to study	-currently represents the largest share of the global market for education services and is growing.
3. Commercial Presence	The provision of a service where the provider establishes, or has presence in, commercial facilities in another country in order to render service.	-local branch or satellite campuses -twinning partnerships -franchising arrangements with local institutions	-increasing interest and strong potential for future growth. -most controversial because it appears to set international rules on foreign investment.
4. Presence of Natural Persons	The provision of a service where people travel to another country on a temporary basis to provide the service.	-professors, teachers, researchers working abroad	-potentially a strong market given the emphasis on mobility of professionals.

Source: Jane Knight, 2006.

identifies these in its Schedule of Specific Commitments. Government commitments to date have ranged from a few to 120 of the approximately 160 service sectors (including sub-sectors).

National Treatment

This facilitates equal treatment for foreign and domestic providers. If once a member country allowed another member to supply a particular service, where specific commitment has made, then it should not discriminate among the foreign and domestic service providers.

Market Access

A negotiated market commitment in specific service sectors. It may be subject to various limitations such as number of service suppliers, values of transactions, total number of service operations, total number of people that may be employed in a particular service sector, and limits on participation of foreign capital. Members are free to tailor sector commitments as they wish, as long as the limits are stated at the outset. They may encounter pressure from other members regarding such limitations. Each member may make additional commitments to provide access beyond the listed measures.

The GATS also contains general obligations relating to transparency of regulations; mutual recognition of the qualifications required for the supply of services; rules governing monopolies and exclusive services suppliers, and other business practices restraining competition.

Significant Features of GATS

GATS is an 'extraordinarily ambitious and quite complex' agreement:

- It is designed to cover all government measures which affect the supply of a service having some international components.
- It covers all service sectors and all modes of supply, but currently apply only to sectors specified by member governments. No discrimination is allowed between profit and not for profit suppliers.
- It expands trade in services constantly and the protection provided in the agreement to members is uncertain and temporary in nature.
- It is effectively unalterable. Once members have made commitments they cannot go back on their commitments.

Category of Education Services

The trade in education is classified into five categories on the basis of the United Nations Provisional Central Product Classification (CPC); the above explained four modes apply to each of the sub-sectors. The Higher education is getting much attention, but the attention should be given for fifth category i.e. "other services". But attention to "other services" is important because this category includes a variety of services of interest to higher education, including testing, language training, student or teacher recruitment, and others (Knight Jane, 2006).

Table 4.2: Classification System for Educational Services

Category of educational service	*Educational activities included in each category*	*Notes*
Primary Education (CPC 921)	Pre-school and other primary education services does not cover child-care services.	—
Secondary Education (CPC 922)	General higher secondary technical and vocational secondary also covers technical and vocational services for the disabled.	—
Higher Education (CPC 923)	Post-secondary technical and vocational education services other higher education services leading to university degree or equivalent.	Types of education (i.e., business, liberal arts, science) are not specified assumes that all post-secondary training and education programmes are covered.
Adult Education (CPC 924)	Covers education for adults outside the regular education system.	Further delineation is needed.
Other Education (CPC 929)	Covers all other education services not elsewhere classified excludes education services related to recreation matters.	Needs clarification recoverage and differentiation from other categories for example—education and language testing services, student recruitment services, quality assessment covered.

Source: Jane Knight, 2002

What Forces are Shaping Trade in Education?

The following major changes in conditions affecting the context of higher education give GATS a potentially critical role in higher education around the world.

- **Globalization:** The Globalization has made the world a small village and the inter-connection and inter-dependence among nations in each activity is increasing; side by side quality and competence have become key factors for survival; consequently demand for higher education is increased in particularly developing countries. Further, it has expanded the mobility of students, labour and capital across borders; as a result, the opportunities and capacities to expand the market for higher education have also increased tremendously. That growth will continue even more rapidly over the next few years. With it come both opportunities and potential threats for Indian higher education. Though the impact in the short run may be limited, the potential long-term consequences are significant. The phenomenon of globalization has increased in number of students going abroad for higher studies, increased in exchange and linkages among faculties and researchers, increased international marketing of curricula and programmes, established branch campuses abroad and increased the academic cooperation across the countries.
- **Information and Communications Technology (ICT):** The rapid worldwide expansion of ICT has reduced the distance among people and nations, and the reduced costs of much of this technology have generated a major expansion in its application to education. Consequently, Distance Learning (Virtual Universities) is getting popularity in spreading education to remote corner of the world. In many parts of the world, ICT holds promise for reaching populations that could not be served by traditional education institutions.
- **Increasing Competition:** Competition among domestic private education providers is being observed from early days; but now it increased to great extent and in recent years, competition from foreign institutions is added to its magnitude particularly in developing countries. This type of competition has provided benefits as well as risks to higher education system; here only concern is about poor and meritorious students and national interest. The WTO regime has increased competition in almost all sectors; education is also not exceptional for that. Further, under GATS education is treated as tradable service; consequently competition is increased among education providers.

Key Dates and Actions of GATS

Table 4.3 highlights about the key dates and actions of GATS

Table 4.3: Key Dates and Actions of GATS

Date	*Action*	*Notes for Education Sector*
1995	GATS founder; initial commitments	44 countries (if you count the EU as one country) made commitments to Education. Of these 44 countries, 21 included commitments to higher education.
End of 2001	Negotiating proposals due	Four countries—USA, Australia, New Zealand and Japan submitted a proposal outlining their general positions related to commitments in the education sector. Japan's proposal was remarkably different as their statement highlighted quality assurance, recognition of credentials and distance education as key issues that required further consideration.
June 2002	All requests for access to foreign markets due	To date, only 34 out of the 145 WTO members have tabled their requests. It is not mandatory for a country to publish their tabled requests for market access in other countries. However, there were leaks and it is known that the USA made substantial requests of other countries to remove barriers to enable greater access to higher, adult and other educational services.
March 2003	Offers from each country to provide access to their domestic market due	As of the end of April 2003, only 20 countries had submitted their offers. Argentina, Australia, Bahrain, Canada, European Union, Hong Kong, Iceland, Israel, Japan, Liechtenstein, New Zealand, Norway, Panama, Poland, Paraguay, South Korea, Switzerland, Taiwan, the United States and Uruguay. It is not necessary for a country to publish their offers and only 8 of the 20 countries have done so to date. These countries are Australia, Canada, European Union, Japan, Llechtenstein, New Zealand, Norway and the United States.
Up to January 1, 2005	Countries can submit offers and requests until end of Doha round	The end date of this round may be extended given the significant delays in the tabling of both requests and offers. Further rounds will occur. It is important to note that offers made during the negotiation phase of the Doha round are conditional up to the conclusion of the negotiating round and at that time, final offers are included in a country's schedule of commitments.

Source: Jane Knight, 2003.

agreement and it is observed that only few members have tabled their requests or offers by the targeted dates.

WTO Member Nations Commitments to Education Under GATS

Table 4.4 gives an idea of type of commitments already made by various member countries on education sector under the GATS agreement. The education sector is divided into five sub-sectors of service; namely, primary, secondary, higher, adult and other. It is observed that, so far 47 countries have made commitments for education under the GATS agreement, but it is interesting to note that, 38 members have tabled their commitments for higher education; it is the highest among all the five levels of education classification. Further, it is found that, only 11 members have committed for all the five levels or classification of education. But India has yet to commit its education sector to GATS.

Status of India's Commitment in Higher Education

India has yet to commit its education sector under GATS framework, the liberalization allowed in the area like allowing 100 per cent FDI on automatic route and permitting foreign participation in higher education is essentially a domestic decision and has not yet been included under the obligations of GATS. Right now only the AICTE has issued a notification that carries revised regulations for the entry and operation of foreign universities/institutions imparting technical education in India; but yet, the Government and related regulatory bodies like the UGC, the MCI, the DCI, the PCI, the BCI, the ICAR etc. have urgently come out with a definite policy/legislation for regulating the entry and operation of foreign institution/university.

The Government of India has constituted the Committee for Promotion of Indian Education Abroad (COPIEA) in April 2002, the Committee performs two important activities viz. promoting of Indian education abroad and regulating operations of foreign educational institutions in India to safeguard the larger national interest and the interest of the student community in particular. Recently, the Government of India has constituted a Committee under the chairmanship of C.N.R. Rao for recommending the policy measures

Table 4.4: GATS Commitments to Education, as of February 2006

Country	*Commitments made at different Educational levels*					
	Primary	*Secondary*	*Higher*	*Adult*	*Other*	*Total*
Albania	X	X	X	X		4
Armenia			X	X		2
Australia		X	X		X	3
Austria	X	X		X		3
Bulgaria	X	X		X		3
Cambodia			X	X	X	3
China	X	X	X	X	X	5
Congo RP			X			1
Costa Rica	X	X	X			3
Croatia		X	X	X	X	4
Czech Republic	X	X	X	X	X	5
Estonia	X	X	X	X	X	5
European Community	X	X	X	X		4
FYR Macedonia	X	X	X	X	X	5
Gambia	X			X	X	3
Georgia	X	X	X	X		4
Ghana		X			X	2
Haiti				X		1
Hungary	X	X	X	X		4
Jamaica	X	X	X			3
Japan	X	X	X	X		4
Jordan	X	X	X	X	X	5
Kyrgyz Republic	X	X	X	X		4
Latvia	X	X	X	X		4
Lesotho	X	X	X	X	X	5
Liechtenstein	X	X	X	X		4
Lithuania	X	X	X	X		4
Mali				X		1
Mexico	X	X	X		X	4
Moldova	X	X	X	X	X	5
Nepal			X	X	X	3
New Zealand	X	X	X			3
Norway	X	X	X	X	X	5
Oman	X	X	X	X		4
Panama	X	X	X			3
Poland	X	X	X	X		4
Rwanda				X		1
Saudi Arabia	X	X	X	X	X	5
Sierra Leone	X	X	X	X	X	5
Slovak Republic	X	X	X	X	X	5
Slovenia		X	X	X		3
Switzerland	X	X	X	X		4
Taiwan China	X	X	X	X		4
Thailand	X	X		X		3
Trinidad & Tobago			X		X	2
Turkey	X	X	X		X	4
USA				X	X	2
Total 47	33	37	38	37	22	167

Source: Knight, 2006.

Note: X – indicates commitment made on different levels of education.

regarding the operation and regulation of foreign universities/ institutions in India; but Committee has yet to submit its report to Government. On the other hand, as India has not committed its education sector to WTO's GATS agreements; but it has received requests from several countries like Australia, Brazil, Japan, New Zealand, Norway, Singapore, and the US. A similar request in higher education services was repeated in the plurilateral negotiations held recently at the WTO.

Conclusion

After glancing over the organizational structure of WTO and GATS; it can be concluded that, the earlier GATT was an international trade organization without any legal recognition; but the WTO is a legal entity; it guides member nations in their trade activities and members are binding to WTO agreements, rules and regulations. The GATS is first ever set of multilateral rules covering international trade services; it is covered and administered by the WTO. The aim of GATS is to promote trade in services; education is also one of those services. All member nations of WTO are covered by GATS; the each member nation has right to determine the extent of its commitments, with each new round of negotiations, members are expected to add sectors or sub-sectors to their national schedules of commitments. As far commitment on education sector under GATS is concerned; out of 150 member nations just 49 nations have made commitment on education sector and among them only 39 nations have committed for higher education. It clearly indicates that education sector in general and higher education sector in particular has huge potentiality to grow in future under GATS. Further, the above explanation and discussion facilitate for comprehending the structure and activities of WTO and GATS agreements; which help us to frame the future policy measures in higher education sector.

5

General Agreement on Trade in Services

An Analysis of Its Agreements and Their Implications on Indian Higher Education

Introduction

The WTOs GATS is the first ever set of multilateral, legally enforceable rules covering trade in continuous liberalization through periodic negotiations. One of the significant features of GATS is that it is effectively irreversible. Once governments have made commitments, they are to all intents and purposes "locked in" and cannot go back from their commitments, or claim exemptions in that area, at a later date. However, governments may be able to modify their scheduled commitments after three years, but they have to compensate all WTO members with substitute commitments, therefore it should be dealt with very cautiously.

The WTO and GATS agreements are multi-disciplinary in nature; they are concerned to many disciplines viz. economics, law (judiciary), polity, geography, science etc. Hence, understanding of WTO and GATS are difficult; due to their complex nature. As GATS is a complex treaty; it does not lay down minimum standards as TRIPS do. Rather, it takes shape through the process of negotiation; means multilateral negotiations of member nations play a crucial role in enhancing trade in services. However, the studying of the GATS articles is prerequisite factor for understanding and making the commitment on higher education sector. In this chapter, WTO's GATS articles are presented and implications of the articles of the agreements on Indian higher education are analyzed.

Structure of GATS Articles

Chart 5.1 provides structural outlook of GATS articles; the GATS has total 29 articles, which are classified into six parts. The part-II i.e. General Obligations and Disciplines are usually applicable to all member nations of the WTO.

A. Part-I (Scope and Definition)

The first part of GATS articles cover only one article i.e. *Scope and Definition*; which explains about the meaning and scope of supply of services i.e. four modes of supply of services; further it highlights the measures which can be taken by the member nations. Below the article 1, i.e. *Scope and Definition's* text is presented and later implications are drawn out.

Article 1: Scope and Definition

1. This Agreement applies to measures by Members affecting trade in services.
2. For the purposes of this Agreement, trade in services is defined as the supply of a service:
   (a) from the territory of one Member into the territory of any other Member;
   (b) in the territory of one Member to the service consumer of any other Member;
   (c) by a service supplier of one Member, through commercial presence in the territory of any other Member;
   (d) by a service supplier of one Member, through presence of natural persons of a Member in the territory of any other Member.
3. For the purposes of this Agreement:
   (a) "measures by Members" means measures taken by:
      (i) central, regional or local governments and authorities; and
      (ii) non-governmental bodies in the exercise of powers delegated by central, regional or local governments or authorities;
      In fulfilling its obligations and commitments under the Agreement, each Member shall take such

Chart 5.1: Articles of GATS†

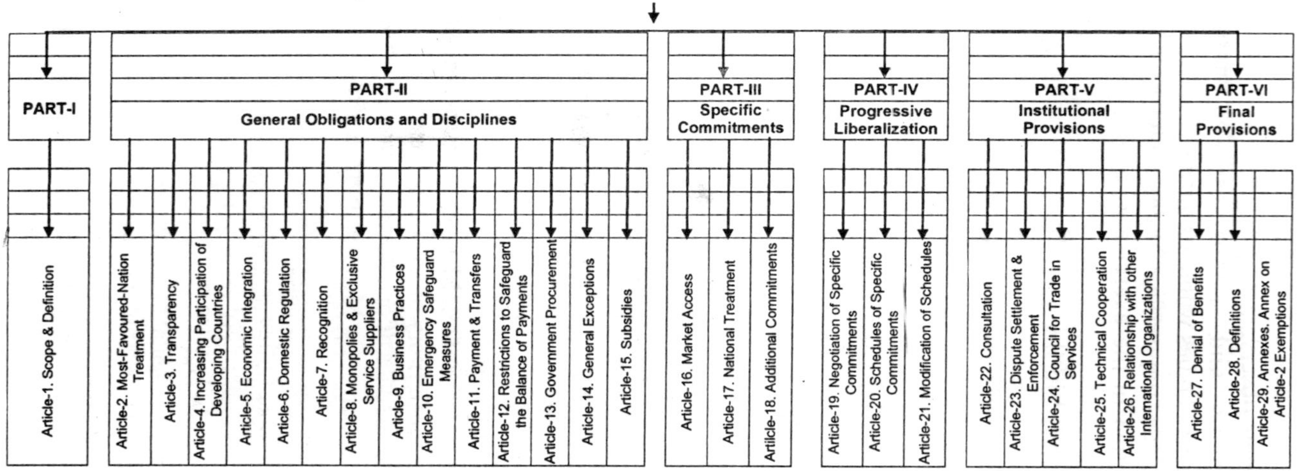

† The textual information of each article of the GATS has been taken from the book: Gupta K.R., *World Trade Organization (Text)*, Atlantic Publishers and Distributors, New Delhi. 2000.

reasonable measures as may be available to it to ensure their observance by regional and local governments and authorities and non-governmental bodies within its territory;

(b) "services" includes any service in any sector except services supplied in the exercise of governmental authority;

(c) "a service supplied in the exercise of governmental authority" means any service which is supplied neither on a commercial basis, nor in competition with one or more service suppliers.

Implications

The GATS facilitates for trade by Indian Universities and higher educational institutes to supply their services for all members of WTO and *vice versa*. Further, the territory of members of WTO becomes a 'free trade zone' for supplying the educational services. In this connection, India can take necessary measures/actions to export and import of educational services. The Indian universities and higher education institutions can trade their educational services through four modes of supply viz. Cross border supply, Consumption abroad, Commercial presence and Presence of natural persons. But it is an arbitrary one; means there is no binding on India to commit higher education for all four modes; on the bases of its preferences India can choose the mode for trade in education services.

B. General Obligations and Disciplines

It is second part of GATS articles; it totally includes 14 articles of GATS and few of them (viz. MFN, Transparency etc.) generally applicable to all member nations; further few articles (viz. Domestic Regulations, Recognition, Subsidies etc.) act as protective measures for member nations. Here article-wise a textual explanation is presented and later an attempt has been made to draw the implications of those articles to Indian higher education sector.

Most-Favoured-Nation Treatment

1. With respect to any measure covered by this Agreement, each Member shall accord immediately and unconditionally to services and service suppliers of any Member treatment no less favourable than that it accords to like services and service suppliers of any other country.
2. A Member may maintain a measure inconsistent with paragraph 1 provided that such a measure is listed in, and meets the conditions of, the Annex on Article II Exemptions.
3. The provisions of this Agreement shall not be so construed as to prevent any member from conferring or according advantages to adjacent countries in order to facilitate exchanges limited to contiguous frontier zones of services that are both locally produced and consumed.

Implications

These general obligations apply automatically to all member nations regardless of the existence of commitments. If India tables its commitment on higher education sector to GATS; then it has to treat one's trading partners equally and this article insists India for granting Most Favoured Nation Treatment (MFN) to all the members of WTO, means if India allows foreign competition (Foreign Universities and Higher Education Institutions) in higher education sector, equal opportunities/treatments in this sector should be given to service providers from all WTO members. On the other hand, if India decides to exclude any particular member nation from providing a higher education service; then all WTO members are excluded.

Sometimes the fake foreign universities may enter Indian higher education sector for exploiting the Indian market. Hence, the regulatory bodies of different courses in higher education such as University Grants Commission (UGC), The National Council of Teachers' Education (NCTE), The All India Council for Technical Education (AICTE), The Medical Council of India (MCI), The Dental Council of India (DCI), The Central Council of Indian Medicine (CCIM), The Indian Council of Medical Research (ICMR), The Indian Nursing Council (INC), The Pharmacy Council of India (PCI), The Bar Council of India (BCI), The Indian Council of Agricultural Research (ICAR), etc. should issue their own regulatory mechanism for the entry and operation of foreign institutions in their respective areas.

Transparency

1. Each Member shall publish promptly and, except in emergency situations, at the latest by the time of their entry into force, all relevant measures of general application which pertain to or affect the operation of this Agreement. International agreements pertaining to or affecting trade in services to which a Member is a signatory shall also be published.
2. Where publication as referred to in paragraph 1 is not practicable, such information shall be made otherwise publicly available.
3. Each Member shall promptly and at least annually inform the Council for Trade in Services (CTS) of the introduction of any new, or any changes to existing laws, regulations or administrative guidelines which significantly affect trade in services covered by its specific commitments under this Agreement.
4. Each Member shall respond promptly to all requests by any other member for specific information on any of its measures of general application or international agreements within the meaning of paragraph 1. Each Member shall also establish one or more enquiry points to provide specific information to other Members, upon request, on all such matters as well as those subject to the notification requirement in paragraph 3. Such enquiry points shall be established within two years from the date of entry into force of the Agreement Establishing the WTO (referred to in this Agreement as the "WTO Agreement"). Appropriate flexibility with respect to the time-limit within which such enquiry points are to be established may be agreed upon for individual developing country Members. Enquiry points need not be depositories of laws and regulations.
5. Any Member may notify to the Council of Trade in Services any measures, taken by any other Member, which it considers affects the operation of this Agreement.

Disclosure of Confidential Information (Article III BIS)

Nothing in the Agreement shall require any Member to provide confidential information, the disclosure of which would impede law enforcement, or otherwise be contrary to the public interest, or which would prejudice legitimate commercial interests of particular enterprises, public or private.

Implications

Under this article, India should publish/make publicly available of its all Acts/Laws /Policies/Programmes/Regulations/Rules/Decisions including relevant international agreements of the higher education sector. The Government of India is required to inform the WTO-CTS of the introduction or amendment of any measures, which affects India's commitments in the area of higher education. India is required to establish one or more 'Enquiry Points' for providing any information pertaining to higher education. In this connection India should be very careful in guarding its sovereignty.

Increasing Participation of Developing Countries

1. The increasing participation of developing country Member in world trade shall be facilitated through negotiated specific commitments, by different Members pursuant to Parts III and IV of this Agreement, relating to:
   (a) the strengthening of their domestic services capacity and its efficiency and competitiveness, *inter alia* through access to technology on a commercial basis;
   (b) the improvement of their access to distribution channels and information networks; and
   (c) the liberalization of market access in sectors and modes of supply of export interest to them.
2. Developed country Members, and to the extent possible other Member, shall establish contact points within two years from the date of entry into force of the WTO Agreement to facilitate the access of developing country Members' service suppliers to information, related to their respective markets, concerning:
   (a) commercial and technical aspects of the supply of services;
   (b) registration, recognition and obtaining of professional qualifications;

(c) the availability of services technology.

3. Special priority shall be given to the least-developed country Members in the implementation of paragraphs 1 and 2. Particular account shall be taken of the serious difficulty of the least-developed countries in accepting negotiated specific commitments in view of their special economic situation and their development, trade and financial needs.

Implications

Basically India belongs to developing countries category, it is essential to tap optimum benefits from Article IV of GATS. India is required to strengthen the domestic services capacity, efficiency and competitiveness of its Universities and Higher Education Institutions through access to technology on a commercial basis. It is necessary for India to improve the access of its Universities and Higher Education Institutions to distribution channels and information networks. India is also required to liberalize its higher education market, where it has comparative advantages over others.

This article make mandatory for developed member nations to establish 'contact points'; it helps developing and least developed country members to get information. In this connection, India may collect as much information as possible from developed countries related to their education markets, concerning:

- Commercial and technical aspects of the supply of services of their Universities and Higher Education Institutions.
- Registration, recognition and obtaining of professional qualifications necessary for exporting Indian education services.
- The availability of services technology in their Universities and Higher Education Institutions.

Economic Integration

1. This Agreement shall not prevent any of its Members from being a party to or entering into an agreement liberalizing trade in services between or among the parties to such an agreement, provided that such an agreement:

   (a) Has substantial sectoral coverage. This condition is

understood in terms of number of sectors, volume of trade affected and modes of supply. In order to meet this condition, agreements should not provide for the *a priori* exclusion of any mode of supply.

(b) Provides for the absence or elimination of substantially all discriminations, in the sense of Article XVII, between or among the parties, in the sectors covered under sub-paragraph (a), through:

(i) elimination of existing discriminatory measures, and/ or

(ii) prohibition of new or more discriminatory measures,

either at the entry into force of that agreement or on the basis of a reasonable time-frame, except for measures permitted under Articles XI, XII, XIV and XIV BIS.

2. In evaluating whether the conditions under paragraph 1(b) are met, consideration may be given to the relationship of the agreement to a wider process of economic integration or trade liberalization among the countries concerned.

3. (a) Where developing countries are parties to an agreement of the type referred to in paragraph 1, flexibility shall be provided for regarding the conditions set out in paragraph 1, particularly with reference to sub-paragraph (b) thereof, in accordance with the level of development of the countries concerned, bother overall and in individual sectors and sub-sectors.

(b) Notwithstanding paragraph 6, in the case of an agreement of the type referred to in paragraph 1 involving only developing countries, more favourable treatment may be granted to juridical persons owned or controlled by natural persons of the parties to such an agreement.

4. Any agreement referred to in paragraph 1 shall be designed to facilitate trade between the parties to the agreement and shall not in respect of any Member outside the agreement raise the overall level of barriers to trade in services within the respective sectors or sub-sectors compared to the level applicable prior to such an agreement.

5. If, in the conclusion, enlargement or any significant modification of any agreement under paragraph 1, a Member

intends to withdraw or modify a specific commitment inconsistently with the terms and conditions set out in its Schedule, it shall provide at least 90 days advance notice of such modification or withdrawal and the procedure set forth in paragraphs 2, 3 and 4 of Article XXI shall apply.

6. A service supplier of any other Member that is a juridical person constituted under the laws of a party to an agreement referred to in paragraph 1 shall be entitled to treatment granted under such agreement, provided that it engages in substantive business operations in the territory of the parties to such agreement.
7. (a) Members which are parties to any agreement referred to in paragraph 1 shall promptly notify any such agreement and any enlargement or any significant modification of that agreement to the Council for Trade in Services. They shall also make available to the Council such relevant information as may be requested by it. The Council may establish a working party to examine such an agreement and to report to the Council on its consistency with this Article.
   (b) Members which are parties to any agreement referred to in paragraph 1 which is implemented on the basis of a time-frame shall report periodically to the Council for Trade in Services on its implementation. The Council may establish a working party to examine such reports if it deems such a working party necessary.
   (c) Based on the reports of the working parties referred to in sub-paragraphs (a) and (b), the Council may make recommendations to the parties as it deems appropriate.
8. A Member which is a party to any agreement referred to in paragraph 1 may not seek compensation for trade benefits that may accrue to any other Member from such agreement.

Labour Market Integration Agreements (Article V BIS)

This Agreement shall not prevent any of its Members from being a party to an agreement establishing full integration. Typically, such integration provides citizens of the parties concerned with a right of free entry to the employment markets of the parties and includes measures concerning conditions of pay, other conditions of employment and social benefits of the labour markets between or among the parties to such an agreement:

(a) exempts citizens of parties to the agreement from requirements concerning residency and work permits;
(b) is notified to the Council for Trade in Services.

Implications

Under this Article India is required to eliminate existing discriminatory measures (tariffs, barriers, quantitative restrictions etc.) as well as prohibit new discriminatory measures for trade in Indian higher education services. The Government of India has to inform WTO-CTS regarding any discriminatory measures and modified measures. This article widens the higher education market through free movement of higher education goods and services.

Taking advantages available under para 3 of Article-V, India can avail concessions. India also taking advantage of this Article may try to eliminate/prohibit discriminatory measures for trade in services in other member countries of WTO. Finally, India may produce a document comprising all the discriminatory measures existing in the sector of Indian Higher Education as well as request WTO to produce a country-by-country report of discriminatory measures for trade in education services.

Domestic Regulation

1. In sectors where specific commitments are undertaken, each Member shall ensure that all measures of general application affecting trade in services are administered in a reasonable, objective and impartial manner.
2. (a) Each Member shall maintain or institute as soon as practicable judicial, arbitral or administrative tribunals or procedures which provide, at the request of an affected service supplier, for the prompt review of, and where justified, appropriate remedies for administrative decisions affecting trade in services. Where such procedures are not independent of the agency entrusted with the administrative decision concerned, the Member shall ensure that the procedures in fact provide for an objective and impartial review.

   (b) The provisions of sub-paragraph (a) shall not be

construed to require a Member to institute such tribunals or procedures where this would be inconsistent with its constitutional structure or the nature of its legal system.

3. Where authorization is required for the supply of a service on which a specific commitment has been made, the competent authorities of a Member shall, within a reasonable period of time after the submission of an application considered complete under domestic laws and regulations, inform the applicant of the decision concerning the application. At the request of the applicant, the competent authorities of the Member shall provide, without undue delay, information concerning the status of the application.

4. With a view to ensuring that measures relating to qualification requirements and procedures, technical standards and licensing requirements do not constitute unnecessary barriers to trade in services, the Council for Trade in Services shall, through appropriate bodies it may establish, develop any necessary disciplines. Such disciplines shall aim to ensure that such requirements are, *inter alia*:
   (a) based on objective and transparent criteria, such as competence and the ability to supply the service;
   (b) not more burdensome that necessary to ensure the quality of the service;
   (c) in the case of licensing procedures, not in themselves a restriction on the supply of the service.

5. (a) In sectors in which a Member has undertaken specific commitments, pending the entry into force of disciplines developed in these sectors pursuant to paragraph 4, the Member shall not apply licensing and qualification requirements and technical standards that nullify or impair such specific commitments in the manner which:
      (i) does not comply with the criteria outlined in sub-paragraphs 4(a), (b) or (c); and
      (ii) could not reasonably have been expected of that Member at the time the specific commitments in those sectors were made.
   (b) In determining whether a Member is in conformity with the obligation under paragraph 5(a), account shall be taken of international standards of relevant international organizations applied by that Member. The term

"relevant international organizations" refers to international bodies whose membership is open to the relevant bodies of at least all Members of the WTO.

6. In sectors where specific commitments regarding professional services are undertaken, each Member shall provide for adequate procedures to verify the competence of professionals of any other Member.

Implications

Government of India is required to establish judicial or quasi-judicial mechanism for providing prompt, objective and impartial justice. Means, if India has made specific commitment on higher education; it shall ensure that all measures that affect trade in higher educational services are administered in a reasonable, objective and impartial manner. For issuing permission for the supply of service of foreign universities and higher education institutions a reasonable procedure and time-frame has to be established; which should be adhered to promptly; the Government of India may follow: qualification requirements, procedures, technical standards and licensing requirement etc. do not constitute unnecessary barriers to trade in services. In one angle this article questions Government of India's regulating power. As Kaushik Madhulika (2004) observed that "The article provides that it must be ensured that "qualification, requirements and procedures, technical standards and licensing are not more burdensome than necessary to ensure the quality of services". The terms "more burdensome than necessary" and "quality of service" have not been defined anywhere in the GATS, hence this is one of the Articles that are still 'under development'. Moreover, there is no clearance about the agency which would determine whether a regulation is 'burdensome' or not, and like this the article, puts an inquiry on Government of India's potential ability to regulate some of the above concerns once the GATS commitments are signed." (Kaushik Madhulika, 2004)

Using Article-VI, India can regulate foreign universities and higher education institutions, which intends to operate in India effectively. These domestic regulations are necessary for promoting objectives of National Education Policies (to attain the aspects of accessibility, quality and equity) and for protecting the public higher education system. Further, domestic regulations control the activities of commercial education institutions and unscrupulous providers in India.

Recognition

1. For the purposes of the fulfilment, in whole or in part, of its standards or criteria for the authorization, licensing or certification of services suppliers, and subject to the requirements of paragraph 3, a Member may recognize the education or experience obtained, requirements met, or licenses or certifications granted in a particular county. Such recognition, which may be achieved through harmonization or otherwise, may be based upon an agreement or arrangement with the country concerned or may be accorded autonomously.
2. A Member that is a party to an agreement or arrangement of the type referred to in paragraph 1, whether existing or future, shall afford adequate opportunity for other interested Members to negotiate their accession to such an agreement or arrangement or to negotiate comparable ones with it. Where a Member accords recognition autonomously, it shall afford adequate opportunity for any other Member to demonstrate that education, experience, licenses, or certifications obtained or requirements met in that other Member's territory should be recognized.
3. A Member shall not accord recognition in a manner which would constitute a means of discrimination between countries in the application of its standards or criteria for the authorization, licensing or certification services suppliers, or a disguised restriction on trade in services.
4. Each Member shall:
   (a) Within 12 months from the date on which the WTO Agreement takes effect for it, inform the Council for Trade in Services of its existing recognition measures and state whether such measures are based on agreements or arrangements of the type referred to in paragraph 1.
   (b) Promptly inform the Council for Trade in Services as far in advance as possible of the opening of negotiations on an agreement or arrangement of the type referred to in paragraph 1 in order to provide adequate opportunity

to any other Member to indicate their interest in participating in the negotiations before they enter a substantive phase.

(c) Promptly inform the Council for Trade in Services when it adopts new recognition measures are based on an agreement or arrangement of the type referred to in paragraph 1.

5. Wherever appropriate, recognition should be based on multilaterally agreed criteria. In appropriate cases, Members shall work in cooperation with relevant inter-governmental and non-governmental organizations towards the establishment and adoption common international standards for the practice of relevant services, trades and professions.

Implications

This article serves the interest of student communities regarding foreign universities recognition in Indian higher education market; here Government of India can act autonomously for recognizing foreign education service suppliers. In this connection Bolashetty Shripad (2005) suggested in his works that the Indian universities and higher education institutions are required to be raised to the level of common international standards and criteria for recognition. The Government of India is required to evolve standards or criteria for; recognizing the educational qualifications/experiences obtained in other countries and licensing or certification of service suppliers of other countries in India.

The Government of India and other member countries have to inform the WTO-CTS existing recognition measure and state whether such measures are based on agreements or arrangements; and date of adoption of new recognition measures.

Already a substantial amount of work is being done on national and international recognition of qualifications. The UNESCO Global Forum on International Quality Assurance, Accreditation and the Recognition of Qualification is currently focused (recognition of qualifications) observed by Anandakrishnan (2004).

Monopolies and Exclusive Service Suppliers

1. Each Member shall ensure that any monopoly supplier of a

service in its territory does not, in the supply of the monopoly service in the relevant market, act in a manner inconsistent with that Member's obligations under Article II and specific commitments.

2. Where a Member's monopoly supplier competes, either directly or through an affiliated company, in the supply of a service outside the scope of its monopoly rights and which is subject to that Member's specific commitments, the Member shall ensure that such a supplier does not abuse its monopoly position to act in its territory in a manner inconsistent with such commitments.
3. The Council for Trade in Services may, at the request of a Member which has a reason to believe that a monopoly supplier of a service of any other Member is acting in a manner inconsistent with paragraph 1 or 2 request the Member establishing, maintaining or authorizing such supplier to provide specific information concerning the relevant operations.
4. If, after the date of entry into force of the WTO Agreement, a Member grants monopoly rights regarding the supply of a service covered by its specific commitments, that Member shall notify the Council for Trade in Services no later than three months before the intended implementation of the grant of monopoly rights and the provisions of paragraphs 2, 3 and 4 of Article XXI shall apply.
5. The provisions of this Article shall also apply to cases of exclusive service suppliers, where a Member, formally or in effect, (a) authorizes or establishes a small number of service suppliers and (b) substantially prevents competition among those suppliers in its territory.

Implications

Under this Article, the Government of India is required to restrict, control and harmonies its domestic monopoly service supplying university or higher education institution (public/private) which may obstruct the spirit of competitiveness and also it become contradictory in tune with Article-II of GATS i.e. MFN Treatment. This article affects government supported public higher education institutions; where government is enjoying monopoly power on higher education; consequently it increases the scope for private operators in higher education system. Nuna Sheel (2004) observed that, strict adherence to the principles of full service liberalization could make abandoning governmental monopolies of higher education an imperative, leading the way to substantial privatization and withdrawal of government support from public institutions of higher education.

If Government of India has committed its higher education sector for GATS agreement and later it has provided monopoly rights to particular higher education institution/university concerning the supply of education services, on such circumstances India should bring in notice (about monopoly establishment, authorization and operations) to the Council for Trade in Services within three months, means before its implementation.

Business Practices

1. Member recognize that certain business practices of service suppliers, other than those falling under Article VIII, may restrain competition and thereby restrict trade in services.
2. Each Member shall, at the request of any other Member, enter into consultations with a view to eliminating practices referred to in paragraph 1. The Member addressed shall accord full and sympathetic consideration to such a request and shall cooperate through the supply of publicly available non-confidential information of relevance to the matter in question. The Member addressed shall also provide other information available to the requesting Member, subject to its domestic law and to the conclusion of satisfactory agreement concerning the safeguarding of its confidentiality by the requesting Member.

Implications

The Government of India is required to recognize and eliminate business practices of any higher education institutions those do not come under Article VIII. Because it holds back the competition among institutions and thereby it restricts trade in educational services. In this connection, if any member countries asked information regarding such practices, then the Government of India and higher education institutions are answerable to the objections raised by member countries in this regard.

Emergency Safeguard Measures

1. There shall be multilateral negotiations on the question of emergency safeguard measures based on the principle of non-discrimination. The results of such negotiations shall enter into effect on a date not later than three years from the date of entry into force of the WTO Agreement.
2. In the period before the entry into effect of the results of the negotiations referred to in paragraph 1, any Member may, notwithstanding the provisions of paragraph 1 of Article XXI, notify the Council on Trade in Services of its intention to modify or withdraw a specific commitment after a period of one year from the date on which the commitment enters into force; provided that the Member shows cause to the Council that the modification or withdrawal cannot await the lapse of the three-year period provided for in paragraph 1 of Article XXI.
3. The provisions of paragraph 2 shall cease to apply three years after the date of entry into force of the WTO Agreement.

Implications

Under this article, the Government of India may evolve the non-discriminatory emergency safeguard measures through multilateral negotiations. The emergency safeguard measures may be implemented within the year 2008 (because WTO-GATS enter into force from 2005 in India). Further, the commitments of specific sector (e.g. higher education) made by India to WTO-GATS may be withdrawn or modified under the measures taken under Article X:1 subject to modification of schedules procedure.

Payments and Transfers

1. Except under the circumstances envisaged in Article XII, a Member shall not apply restrictions on international transfers and payments for current transactions relating to its specific commitments.
2. Nothing in this Agreement shall affect the rights and obligations of the members of the International Monetary Fund under the Article of Agreement of the Fund, including

the use of exchange actions which are in conformity with the Articles of Agreement, provided that a Member shall not impose restrictions on any capital transactions inconsistently with its specific commitments regarding such transactions, except under Article XII or at the request of the Fund.

Implications

The Government of India and other statutory authorities cannot apply restrictions on 'international transfers and payments' for transactions relating to educational services (specific commitments), but restrictions are applied on such transactions of educational services which comes under Article XII.

Restrictions to Safeguard the Balance of Payments

1. In the event of serious balance-of-payments and external financial difficulties or threat thereof, a Member may adopt or maintain restrictions on trade in services on which it has undertaken specific commitments, including on payments or transfers for transactions related to such commitments. It is recognized that particular pressures on the balance of payments of a Member in the process of economic development or economic transition may necessitate the use of restrictions to ensure, *inter alia*, the maintenance of a level of financial reserves adequate for the implementation of its programme of economic development or economic transition.
2. The restrictions referred to in paragraph 1:
   (a) shall not discriminate among Members;
   (b) shall be consistent with the Articles of Agreement of the International Monetary Fund;
   (c) shall avoid unnecessary damage to the commercial, economic and financial interests of any other Member;
   (d) shall not exceed those necessary to deal with the circumstances described in paragraph 1;
   (e) shall be temporary and be phased out progressively as the situation specified in paragraph 1 improves.
3. In determining the incidence of such restrictions, Members may give priority to the supply of services which are more essential to their economic or development programmes.

However, such restrictions shall not be adopted or maintained for the purpose of protecting a particular service sector.

4. Any restrictions adopted or maintained under paragraph 1, or any changes therein, shall be promptly notified to the General Council.

5. (a) Members applying the provisions of this Article shall consult promptly with the Committee on Balance-of-Payments Restrictions on restrictions adopted under this Article.

   (b) The Ministerial Conference shall establish procedures under paragraph 5 shall be the same as the GATT 1994 procedures for periodic consultations with the objective of enabling each recommendations to be made to the Member concerned as it may deem appropriate.

   (c) Such consultations shall assess the balance-of-payment situation of the Member concerned and the restrictions adopted or maintained under this Article, taking into account, *inter alia*, such factors as:

      (i) the nature and extent of the balance-of-payments and the external financial difficulties;

      (ii) the external economic and trading environment of the consulting Member;

      (iii) alternative corrective measures which may be available.

   (d) The consultations shall address the compliance of any restrictions with paragraph 2, in particular the progressive phase out of restrictions in accordance with paragraph 2(e).

   (e) In such consultations, all findings of statistical and other facts presented by the International Monetary Fund relating to foreign exchange, monetary reserves and balance-of-payments shall be accepted and conclusions shall be based on the assessment by the Fund of the balance-of-payments and the external financial situation of the consulting Member.

   (f) If a Member which is not a member of the International Monetary Fund wishes to apply the provisions of this Article, the Ministerial Conference shall establish a review procedure and any other procedures necessary.

Implications

After committing higher education to GATS, if India faces any external financial difficulties or Balance of Payment (BOP) crisis, then it can adopt restrictions on trade in educational services, including on payments or transfers for transactions related to such commitment prior to consultation with WTO-Committee on BOP Restrictions. The restrictions implemented shall be temporary in nature and not discriminate among members; shall not damage to the commercial, economic and financial interests of any other Member; and reliable with the article of agreement of the IMF and the implemented restrictions and any changes shall be notified to General Council.

Government Procurement

1. Articles II, XVI and XVII shall not apply to laws, regulations or requirements governing the procurement by governmental agencies of services purchased for governmental purposes and not with a view to commercial resale or with a view to use in the supply of services for commercial sale.
2. There shall be multilateral negotiations on government procurement in services under this Agreement within two years from the date of entry into force of the WTO Agreement.

Implications

This article attempts to uphold the 'sovereignty' of the Government, the Government of India for its non-commercial use can procure any educational services by enacting laws or regulations. For these procurement by governmental agencies the articles viz. Most Favoured Treatment (MFN), Market Access and National Treatment will not apply, because these arc used for governmental purposes and not used in the supply of services for commercial sale.

General Exceptions

Subject to the requirement that such measures are not applied in a manner which would constitute a means of arbitrary or unjustifiable discrimination between countries where like conditions prevail, or a disguised restriction on trade in services, nothing in this Agreement shall be construed to prevent the adoption or enforcement by any Member of measures:

(a) necessary to protect public morals or to maintain public order; the public order exception may be invoked only where a genuine and sufficiently serious threat is posed to one of the fundamental interests of society.
(b) necessary to protect human, animal or plant life or health;
(c) necessary to secure compliance with laws or regulations which are not inconsistent with provisions of this Agreement including those relating to:
   (i) the prevention of deceptive and fraudulent practices or to deal with the effects of a default on services contracts;
   (ii) the protection of the privacy of individuals in relation to the processing and dissemination of personal data and the protection of confidentiality of individual records and accounts;
   (iii) safety;
(d) inconsistent with Article XVII, provided that the difference in treatment is aimed at ensuring the equitable or effective measures that are aimed at ensuring the equitable or effective imposition or collection of direct taxes include measures taken by a Member under its taxation system which:
   (i) apply to non-resident service suppliers in recognition of the fact that the tax obligation of non-residents is determined with respect to taxable items sourced or located in the Member's territory; or
   (ii) apply to non-resident in order to ensure the imposition or collection of taxes in the Member's territory; or
   (iii) apply to non-residents or residents in order to prevent the avoidance or evasion of taxes, including compliance measures; or
   (iv) apply to consumers of services supplied in or from the territory of another Member in order to ensure the imposition or collection of taxes on such consumers derived from sources in the Member's territory; or
   (v) distinguish service suppliers subject to tax on worldwide taxable items from other service suppliers, in recognition of the difference in the difference in the nature of the tax base between them; or

(vi) determine, allocate or apportion income, profit, gain, loss, deduction or credit of resident persons or branches, or between related persons or branches of the same person, in order to safeguard the Member's tax base.

Tax terms or concepts in paragraph (d) of Article XIV and in this footnote are determined according to tax definitions and concepts, or equivalent or similar definitions and concepts, under the domestic law of the Member taking the measure, imposition or collection of direct taxes in respect of services or service suppliers of other Members;

(e) inconsistent with Article II, provided that the difference in treatment is the result of an agreement on the avoidance of double taxation or provisions on the avoidance of double taxation in any other international agreement or arrangement by which the Member is bound.

Security Exceptions (Article XIV BIS)

1. Nothing in this Agreement shall be construed:
   (a) to require any Member to furnish any information, the disclosure of which it considers contrary to its essential security interests; or
   (b) to prevent any Member from taking any action which it considers necessary for the protection of its essential security interests:
      (i) relating to the supply of services as carried out directly or indirectly for the purpose of provisioning a military establishment;
      (ii) relating to fissionable and fusionable materials or the materials from which they are derived;
      (iii) taken in time of war or other emergency in international relations; or
   (c) to prevent any Member from taking any action in pursuance of its obligations under the United Nations Charter for the maintenance of international peace and security.
2. The Council for Trade in Services shall be informed to the fullest extent possible of measures taken under paragraphs 1(b) and (c) and of their termination.

Implications

Under this article, the Government of India can adopt some measures for protecting the interest of nation, public, environment and law etc; subsequently nobody (other members) can question these matters, means article XIV allow for exceptions to be made for measures which are meant to protect public order and morals, to protect individuals, and to check professional misconduct, among other concerns. Thus, regulations and policies which are meant to address public concerns (as discussed in the preceding sections) are exempt from market access and national treatment obligations, subject to the condition that they are used in a non-discriminatory manner and are not used as disguised restrictions on trade in services. Further, the objective (accessibility and equity) of National Education Policy (NEP) can be achieved and finally the Government of India has to inform WTO-CTS regarding all measures taken under this article.

Subsidies

1. Members recognize that, in certain circumstances, subsidies may have distortive effects on trade in services. Members shall enter into negotiations with a view to developing the necessary multilateral disciplines to avoid such trade-distortive effects. A future work progamme shall determine how, and in what time-frame, negotiations on such multilateral disciplines will be conducted. The negotiations shall also address the appropriateness of countervailing procedures. Such negotiations shall recognize the role of subsidies in relation to the development programmes of developing countries and take into account the needs of Members, particularly developing country Members, for flexibility in this area. For the purpose of such negotiations, Members shall exchange information concerning all subsidies related to trade in services that they provide to their domestic service suppliers.
2. Any Member which considers that it is adversely affected by a subsidy of another Member may request consultations with that Member on such matters. Such requests shall be accorded sympathetic consideration.

Implications

Government of India, all State Governments are required to prepare in detail an exhaustive information of all subsidies provided to schools/colleges/universities/educational institutions and exchange the same with other members of WTO. The subsidies may have distortive effect on trade in educational services; hence negotiations will be conducted and there members (Government of India) exchange information concerning all subsidies relating to trade in educational services; and take measures to counter trade destructive effect of these subsidies. Further, the Government of India and State Governments would have either to extend the full range of subsidization to foreign affiliates, or cut off these subsidies for domestic institutions. It may lead to fundamental change and far reaching consequences in the system of higher education.

As providing subsidies to local bodies would be considered as barrier to foreign education providers; it alleviates and stops government support (subsidies) for domestic public education institutions. Nuna Sheel (2004) observed that it is hard to think of any nation that does not engage in substantial subsidization of local institutions of higher education.

C. Specific Commitments

This is third part of GATS articles; it includes three important articles of GATS and these articles facilitate the member nations for determining the size of market; where the commitments have already made in particular (higher education) service sector.

Market Access

1. With respect to market access through the modes of supply identified in Article I, each Member shall accord services and service suppliers of any other Member treatment no less favourable than that provided for under the terms, limitations and conditions agreed and specified in its Schedule. If a Member undertakes a market-access commitment in relation to the supply of a service through the mode of supply referred to in sub-paragraph 2(a) of Article I and if the cross-border movement of capital is an essential part of the service itself,

that Member is thereby committed to allow such movement of capital. If a Member undertakes a market-access commitment in relation to the supply of a service through the mode of supply referred to in sub-paragraph 2(c) of Article I, it is thereby committed to allow related transfers of capital into its territory.

2. In sectors where market-access commitments are undertaken, the measures which a Member shall not maintain or adopt either on the basis of a regional sub-division or on the basis of its entire territory, unless otherwise specified in its Schedule, are defined as:
   (a) limitations on the number of service suppliers whether in the form of numerical quotas, monopolies, exclusive service suppliers or the requirements of an economic needs test;
   (b) limitations on the total value of service transactions or assets in the form of numerical quotas or the requirement of an economic needs test;
   (c) limitations on the total number of service operations or on the total quantity of service output expressed in terms of designated numerical units in the form of quotas or the requirement of an economic needs test; Sub-paragraph 2(c) does not cover measures of a Member which limit inputs for the supply of services;
   (d) limitations on the total number of natural persons that may be employed in a particular service sector or that a service supplier may employ and who are necessary for, and directly related to, the supply of a specific service in the form of numerical quotas or the requirement of an economic needs test;
   (e) measures which restrict or require specific types of legal entity or joint venture through which a service supplier may supply a service; and
   (f) limitations on the participation of foreign capital in terms of maximum percentage limit on foreign shareholding or the total value of individual or aggregate foreign investment.

Implications

Under this article, the Government of India can fix and grant the degree of market access to foreign universities/higher education institutions and education service suppliers in Indian higher education sector. This article facilitates India to determine its limitations on market access for higher education sector, hence 'Market Access' is subject to one or six types of limitations defined by GATS agreement.

India can use the following types of limitations for determining the modes of supply of higher education services: number of foreign education service suppliers, values of transactions, total number of educational service operations, total number of people that may be employed in a education service sector, limits on participation of FDI and recognition of qualifications. Further, the Government of India may impose particular limitations such as, the foreign universities/higher education providers compulsorily use local partners; voluntary basis entering into and exiting from joint ventures with local or non-local partners will be restricted, putting ownership limitations on joint ventures with local partners etc. Ultimately, Market Access article play crucial role in determining the scope of specific (e.g. higher education) service market.

National Treatment

1. In the sectors inscribed in its Schedule, and subject to any conditions and qualifications set out therein, each Member shall accord to services and service suppliers of any other Member, in respect of all measures affecting the supply of services, treatment no less favourable than it accords to its own like services and service suppliers. Specific commitments assumed under this Article shall not be construed to require any Member to compensate for any inherent competitive disadvantages which result from the foreign character of the relevant services or service suppliers.
2. A Member may meet the requirement of paragraph 1 by according to services and service suppliers of any other Member, either formally identical treatment or formally different to that it accords to its own like services and service suppliers.
3. Formally identical or formally different treatment shall be considered to be less favourable if it modifies the conditions of competition in favour of services or service suppliers of the Member compared to like services or service suppliers of any other Member.

Implications

Basically this article applies to those countries, which have made specific commitment to particular sector. If India has made specific commitment on higher education under GATS, than the Government of India should (under compulsion) provide equal treatment for foreign higher education institutions as well as Indian higher education institutions. Differential and discriminatory treatment to foreign educational providers in comparison to domestic educational providers will be unfair and against GATS. Hence, Government of India has to evaluate the things very cautiously regarding the pros and cons of the article 'National Treatment' for higher education sector under the GATS, because critics of GATS apprehended that national treatment article could put education under threat as a 'public good'.

Additional Commitments

Member may negotiate commitments with respect to measures affecting trade in services not subject to scheduling under Articles XVI or XVII, including those regarding qualification, standards or licensing matters. Such commitments shall be inscribed in a Member's Schedule.

Implications

The Government of India required maintaining a schedule containing 'its commitments' under GATS. The Government of India can negotiate the matters, which are affecting trade in educational services and those matters may fall outside the schedule of market access, national treatment, educational qualification, standards and licensing matters.

D. Progressive Liberalization

It is fourth part of GATS articles; it also includes three articles. With the help of these articles members can modify the sector, where they have already made commitment on it with subject to certain conditions and regulations of WTO and GATS.

Negotiation of Specific Commitments

1. In pursuance of the objectives of this Agreement, Members

shall enter into successive rounds of negotiations, beginning not later than five years from the date of entry into force of the WTO Agreement and periodically thereafter, with a view to achieving a progressively higher level of liberalization. Such negotiations shall be directed to the reduction or elimination of the adverse effects on trade in services of measures as a means of providing effective market access. This process shall take place with a view to promoting the interests of all participants on a mutually advantageous basis and to securing an overall balance of rights and obligations.

2. The process of liberalization shall take place with due respcct for national policy objectives and the level of development of individual Members, both overall and in individual sectors. There shall be appropriate flexibility for individual developing country Member for opening fewer sectors, liberalizing fewer types of transactions, progressively extending market access in line with their development situation and, when making access to their markets available to foreign service suppliers, attaching to such access conditions aimed at achieving the objectives referred to in Article IV.
3. For each round, negotiating guidelines and procedures shall be established. For the purposes of establishing such guidelines, the Council for Trade in Services shall carry out an assessment of trade in services in overall terms and on a sectoral basis with reference to the objectives of this Agreement, including those set out in paragraph 1 of Article VI. Negotiating guidelines shall establish modalities for the treatment of liberalization undertaken autonomously by Members since pervious negotiations, as well as for the special treatment for least-developed country Members under the provisions of paragraph 3 of Article IV.
4. The process of progressive liberalization shall be advanced in each such round through bilateral, plurilateral or multilateral negotiations directed towards increasing the general level of specific commitments undertaken by Members under this Agreement.

Implications

This article facilitates India to achieve the progressive elimination of tariffs and other barriers in education sector. While there is no time limit on GATS, Government of India is required to participate in successive and periodical rounds of service negotiations with the aim of achieving progressively higher levels of trade rule liberalization. The Government of India may evaluate carefully the pros and cons of progressive and higher level of liberalization of its educational market as well as prepare strategies to safeguard India's interests. In this connection, Government of India may employ Expert Team on Education Service Sector to assist and advise the government on entering into commitments under GATS.

Schedules of Specific Commitments

1. Each Member shall set out in a schedule the specific commitments it undertakes under Part III of this Agreement. With respect to sectors where such commitments are undertaken, each Schedule shall specify:
   (a) terms, limitations and conditions on market access;
   (b) conditions and qualifications on national treatment;
   (c) undertakings relating to additional commitments;
   (d) where appropriate the time-frame for implementation of such commitments; and
   (e) the date of entry into force of such commitments.
2. Measures inconsistent with both Articles XVI and XVII shall be inscribed in the column relating to Article XVI. In this case the inscription will be considered to provide a condition or qualification to Article XVII as well.
3. Schedules of specific commitments shall be annexed to this Agreement and shall form an integral part thereof.

Implications

Under this article, the Government of India is required to prepare a schedule specifying the Commitments undertaken by it under GATS.

In case of the schedule of Educational Commitments should contain:

(a) terms, limitations and conditions on market access for foreign universities and higher education institutions.
(b) conditions and qualifications on national treatment for foreign universities and higher education institutions.

(c) undertaking related to additional educational commitments.
(d) the date of entry into force of educational commitment.

The writing in this article provides a provision to conflicting measures with 'Market Access' and 'National Treatment'.

Modification of Schedules

1. (a) A Member (referred to in this Article as the "modifying Member") may modify or withdraw any commitment in its Schedule, at any time after three years have elapsed from the date on which that commitment entered into force, in accordance with the provisions of this Article.
   (b) A modifying Member shall notify its intent to modify or withdraw a commitment pursuant to this Article to the Council for Trade in Services no later than three months before the intended date of implementation of the modification or withdrawal.
2. (a) At the request of any Member the benefits of which under this Agreement may be affected (referred to in this Article as an "affected Member") by a proposed modification or withdrawal notified under sub-paragraph 1(b), the modifying Member shall enter into negotiations with a view to reaching agreement on any necessary compensatory adjustment. In such negotiations and agreement, the Members concerned shall endeavour to maintain a general level of mutually advantageous commitments not less favourable to trade than that provided for in Schedules of specific commitments prior to such negotiations.
   (b) Compensatory adjustments shall be made on a most-favoured-nation basis.
3. (a) If agreement is not reached between the modifying Member and any affected Member before the end of the period provided for negotiations, such affected Member may refer the matter to arbitration. Any affected Member that wishes to enforce a right that it may have to compensation must participate in the arbitration.
   (b) If no affected Member has requested arbitration, the modifying Member shall be free to implement the proposed modification or withdrawal.

4. (a) The modifying Member may not modify or withdraw its commitment until it has made compensatory adjustments in conformity with the findings of the arbitration.
   (b) If the modifying Member implements its proposed modification or withdrawal and does not comply with the findings of the arbitration, any affected Member that participated in the arbitration may modify or withdraw substantially equivalent benefits in conformity with those findings. Notwithstanding Article II, such a modification or withdrawal may be implemented solely with respect to the modifying Member.
5. The Council for Trade in Services shall establish procedures for rectification or modification of Schedules. Any Member which has modified or withdrawn scheduled commitments under this Article shall modify its Schedule according to such procedures.

Implications

There is a provision under this article that, any member nation (Government of India) can modify or withdraw its educational commitment after three years from the date it entered into force and the withdrawn country has to explain the purpose to the Council for Trade in Services before three months of implementation date of modification/withdrawal. It implies that modification/withdrawal facility provided by GATS is very difficult one than entry. Similar observation is made by Bolashetty Shripad (2005) i.e. the modification/withdrawal process provides for a 'difficult exit route'. The exit from GATS is difficult than entry into GATS. Compensatory adjustments shall be made on a most-favoured-nation basis to affected members. If agreement is not reached among two parties than affected party may refer the matter to WTO-CTS.

E. Institutional Provisions

It is fifth part of GATS articles and covers five articles; explains about the facilities (provisions) available for member nations viz. any developing member nation can get technical assistance from 'contact points'; member can solve their disputes through dispute settlement body and even member can acquire information regarding higher education from United Nations agencies etc.

Consultation

1. Each Member shall accord sympathetic consideration to, and shall afford adequate opportunity for, consultation regarding such representations as may be made by any other Member with respect to any matter affecting the operation of this Agreement. The Dispute Settlement Understanding (DSB) shall apply to such consultations.
2. The Council for Trade in Services or the Dispute Settlement Body (DSB) may, at the request of a Member, consult with any Member or Members in respect of any matter for which it has not been possible to find a satisfactory solution through consultation under paragraph 1.
3. A Member may not invoke Article XVII, either under this Article or Article XXIII, with respect to a measure of another Member that falls within the scope of an international agreement between them relating to the avoidance of double taxation. In case of disagreement between Members as to whether a measure falls within the scope of such an agreement between them, it shall be open to either Member to bring this matter before the Council for Trade in Services. With respect to agreements on the avoidance of double taxation which exist on the date of entry into force of the WTO Agreement, such a matter may be brought before the Council for Trade in Services only with the consent of both parties to such an agreement. The Council shall refer the matter to arbitration. The decision of the arbitrator shall be final and binding on the Members.

Implications

The Government of India can enter into or modify or withdraw any commitment in a manner that does not affect other members of WTO. If any measure/action/step taken by the Government of India affects the interest/benefit of other member, and then under Article XXII a 'consultation mechanism' is evolved. The WTO-CTS negotiate the two parties and outcome of negotiation will be final and binding on the members. If India entry into GATS, consequently Indian Educational institutions are duty-bound to carrying of obligations and fulfilment of commitments.

Dispute Settlement and Enforcement

1. If any Member should consider that any other Member fails to carry out its obligations or specific commitments under this Agreement, it may with a view to reaching a mutually satisfactory resolution of the matter have recourse to the DSU.
2. If the DSB considers that the circumstances are serious enough to justify such action, it may authorize a Member or Members to suspend the application to any other Member or Members of obligations and specific commitments in accordance with Article XXII of the DSU.
3. If any Member considers that any benefit it could reasonably have expected to accrue to it under a specific commitment of another Member under Part III of this Agreement is being nullified or impaired as a result of the application of any measure which does not conflict with the provisions of this Agreement, it may have recourse to the DSU. If the measure is determined by the DSB to have nullified or impaired such a benefit, the Member affected shall be entitled to a mutually satisfactory adjustment on the basis of paragraph 2 of Article XXI, which may include the modification or withdrawal of the measure. In the event an agreement cannot be reached between the Members concerned, Article XXII of the DSU shall apply.

Implications

Under this article, the Dispute Settlement Board resolves the disputes among member nations, the Government of India and other member of WTO are at liberty to enter into bilateral, multilateral or plurilateral 'Dispute Settlement Understanding' in case of failure to carry forward the obligations and fulfilment of commitments. If the Government of India incur losses due to the Withdrawal/Modification of commitment by another member regarding education services, DSB resolve the issue.

Council for Trade in Services

1. The Council for Trade in Services shall carry out such functions as may be assigned to it to facilitate the operation of this Agreement and further its objectives. The Council

may establish such subsidiary bodies as it considers appropriate for the effective discharge of its functions.

2. The Council and, unless the Council decides otherwise, its subsidiary bodies shall be opened to participation by representatives of all Members.
3. The Chairman of the Council shall be elected by the Members.

Implications

The Council for Trade in Services oversees the implementation of all the agreements relating to trade in services and it carry out the functions of implementation of 12 specified services; where educational services is one of them. If necessitate it establishes its subsidiary bodies for discharging the functions. The representatives from India participate in WTO-CTS and its subsidiary bodies. If Government of India would commit higher education to GATS, than it has to communicate with WTO-CTS regarding the developments and changes, matter of dissatisfaction, losses etc. of higher education sector.

Technical Cooperation

1. Service suppliers of Members which are in need of such assistance shall have access to the services of contact points referred to in paragraph 2 of Article IV.
2. Technical assistance to developing countries shall be provided at the multilateral level by the Secretariat and shall be decided upon by the Council for Trade in Services.

Implications

India belongs to developing countries category; it can access any type of technical assistance to their educational institutions/ universities from WTO Secretariat and Council for Trade in Services (WTO-CTS). The Government of India can access assistance and cooperation regarding higher educational services from 'Contact Points' which were established by developed member countries.

Relationship with Other International Organizations

The General Council shall make appropriate arrangements for

consultation and cooperation with the United Nations and its specialized agencies as well as with other intergovernmental organizations concerned with services.

Implications

Government of India can access information regarding higher education from United Nations agencies like UNESCO and other intergovernmental organizations through the WTO-General Council; it can pave direction for Indian Universities and Higher Education Institutions by means of arrangements for consultation and cooperation with such agencies.

F. Final Provisions

It is last part of GATS articles text; includes definitions regarding technical terms viz. Measures, Supply of Services, Commercial presence, Natural Persons, Judicial Persons etc.

Denial of Benefits

A Member may deny the benefits of this Agreement:

(a) to the supply of a service, if it establishes that the service is supplied from or in the territory of a non-Member or of a Member to which the denying Member does not apply the WTO Agreement;

(b) in the case of the supply of a maritime transport service, if it establishes that service is supplied:

  (i) by a vessel registered under the laws of a non-Member or of a Member to which the denying Member does not apply the WTO Agreement, and

  (ii) by a person which operates and/or uses the vessel in whole or in part but which is of a non-Member or of a Member to which the denying Member does not apply the WTO Agreement;

(c) to a service supplier that is a juridical person, if it establishes that it is not a service supplier of another Member, or that it is a service supplier of a Member to which the denying Member does not apply the WTO Agreement.

Implications

Government of India can deny the benefits of GATS to Educational Institutions of Non-members of WTO and Non-signatories of GATS.

Definitions

For the purpose of this Agreement:

(a) "measure" means any measure by a Member, whether in the form of a law, regulation, rule, procedure, decision, administrative action, or any other form;
(b) "supply of a service" includes the production, distribution, marketing, sale and delivery of a service;
(c) "measures by Members affecting trade in services" include measures in respect of—
  (i) the purchase, payment or use of a service;
  (ii) the access to and use of, in connection with the supply of a service, services which are required by those Members to be offered to the public generally;
  (iii) the presence, including commercial presence, of persons of a Member for the supply of a service in the territory of another Member,
(d) "commercial presence" means any type of business or professional establishment, including through—
  (i) the constitution, acquisition or maintenance of a juridical person, or
  (ii) the creation or maintenance of a branch or a representative office,
  within the territory of a Member for the purpose of supplying a service;
(e) "sector" of a service means—
  (i) with reference to a specific commitment, one or more, or all, sub-sectors of that service, as specified in a Member's Schedule,
  (ii) otherwise, the whole of that service sector, including all of its sub-sectors;
(f) "service of another Member" means a service which is supplied,

(i) from or in the territory of that other Member, or in the case of maritime transport, by a vessel registered under the laws of that other Member, or by a person of that other Member which supplies the service through the operation of a vessel and/or its use in whole or in part; or

(ii) in the case of the supply of a service through commercial presence or through the presence of natural persons, by a service supplier of that other Member;

(g) "service supplier" means any person that supplies a service; Where the service is not supplied directly by a juridical person but through other forms of commercial presence such as a branch or a representative office, the service supplier (i.e. the juridical person) shall, nonetheless, through such presence be accorded the treatment provided for service suppliers under the Agreement. Such treatment shall be extended to the presence through which the service is supplied and need not be extended to any other parts of the supplier located outside the territory where the service is supplied.

(h) "monopoly supplier of a service" means any person, public or private, which in the relevant market of the territory of a Member is authorized or established formally or in effect by that Member as the sole supplier of that service;

(i) "service consumer" means any person that receives or uses a service;

(j) "person" means either a natural person or a juridical person;

(k) "natural person of another Member" means a natural person who resides in the territory of that other Member or any other Member, and who under the law of that other Member:

(i) is a national of that other Member; or

(ii) has the right of permanent residence in that other Member, in the case of a Member which:

1. does not have nationals; or
2. accords substantially the same treatment to its permanent residents as it does to its nationals in respect of measures affecting trade in services, as notified in its acceptance of or accession to the WTO Agreement, provided that no Member is obligated to accord to such permanent residents

treatment more favourable than would be accorded by that other Member to such permanent residents. Such notification shall include the assurance to assume, with respect to those permanent residents, in accordance with its laws and regulations, the same responsibilities that other Member bears with respect to its nationals;

(l) "juridical person" means any legal entity duly constituted or otherwise organized under applicable law, whether for profit or otherwise, and whether privately-owned or governmentally-owned, including any corporation, trust, partnership, joint venture, sole proprietorship or association;

(m) "juridical person of another Member" means a juridical person which is either:

   (i) constituted or otherwise organized under the law of that other Member, and is engaged in substantive business operations in the territory of that Member or any other Member; or

   (ii) in the case of the supply of a service through commercial presence, owned or controlled by:

      1. natural persons of that Member; or
      2. juridical persons of that other Member identified under sub-paragraph (i);

(n) a juridical person is:

   (i) "owned" by persons of a Member if more than 50 per cent of the equity interest in it is beneficially owned by persons of that Member;

   (ii) "controlled" with persons of a Member if such persons have the power to name a majority of its directors or otherwise to legally direct its actions;

   (iii) "affiliated" with another person when it controls, or is controlled by, that other person; or when it and the other person are both controlled by the same person;

(l) "direct taxes" comprise all taxes on total income, on total capital or on elements of income or of capital, including taxes on gains from the alienation of property, taxes on estates, inheritances and gifts, and taxes on the total amounts of wages or salaries paid by enterprises, as well as taxes on capital appreciation.

Annex on Article II Exemptions (Annexes)

Scope

1. This Annex specifies the conditions under which a Member, at the entry into force of this Agreement, is exempted from its obligations under paragraph 1 of Article II.
2. Any new exemptions applied for after the date of entry into force of the WTO Agreement shall be dealt with under paragraph 3 of Article IX of that Agreement.

Review

3. The Council for Trade in Services (CTS) shall review all exemptions granted for a period of more than 5 years. The first such review shall take place not more than 5 years after the entry into force of the WTO Agreement.
4. The Council for Trade in Services in a review shall:
   (a) examine whether the conditions which created the need for the exemption still prevail; and
   (b) determine the date of any further review.

Termination

5. The exemption of a Member from its obligations under paragraph 1 of Article II of the Agreement with respect to a particular measure terminates on the date provided for in the exemption.
6. In principle, such exemptions should not exceed a period of 10 years. In any event, they shall be subject to negotiation in subsequent trade liberalizing rounds.
7. A Member shall notify the Council for Trade in Services at the termination of the exemption period that the inconsistent measure has been brought into conformity with paragraph 1 of Article II of the Agreement.

Annex on Movement of Natural Persons Supplying Services under the Agreement

1. This Annex applies to measures affecting natural persons

who are service suppliers of a Member, and natural persons of a Member who are employed by a service supplier of a Member, in respect of the supply of a service.

2. The Agreement shall not apply to measures affecting natural persons seeking access to the employment market of a Member, nor shall it apply to measures regarding citizenship, residence or employment on a permanent basis.
3. In accordance with Parts III and IV of the Agreement, Members may negotiate specific commitments applying to the movement of all categories of natural persons supplying services under the Agreement. Natural persons covered by a specific commitment shall be allowed to supply the service in accordance with the terms of that commitment.
4. The Agreement shall not prevent a Member from applying measures to regulate the entry of natural persons into, or their temporary stay in, its territory, including those measures necessary to protect the integrity of, and to ensure the orderly movement of natural persons across, its borders, provided that such measures are not applied in such a manner as to nullify or impair the benefits accruing to any Member under the terms of a specific commitment. The sole fact of requiring a visa for natural persons of certain Members and not for those of others shall not be regarded as nullifying or impairing benefits under a specific commitment.

Implications

The Annex to this Agreement is an integral part of GATS Agreement; it defines the scope of mode 4 to cover persons who are temporarily working in another member country. It is not applicable to persons who are seeking access to the employment market of another member on a permanent basis or for citizenship purposes. Two categories of service persons viz. independent and self-employed suppliers are covered, who get paid directly by their customers and natural persons who are employed by their service suppliers in the host or home member country in respect to the supply of a service. The annex states that countries can regulate entry and stay of natural persons provided they do not apply these measures in such a manner as to nullify or impair the benefits granted to members under their specific commitments.

India benefit significantly where it has large pool of skilled and semi-skilled human resource e.g. teachers, professors, researchers, lab technicians etc. can move to overseas countries on temporary basis. But at the same time, these individuals will face some regulations while moving to overseas countries.

Conclusion

The foregoing analysis and implications of GATS articles reveals that, articles viz. 'Domestic Regulation', 'Recognition', 'Market Access', 'Subsidies' will provide much scope to Government of India for maintaining the objectives of National Policy of Education; indeed protects the interest of student community. The role of domestic regulation has been clearly recognized for ensuring equity, quality, accessibility, consumer protection, standards etc. in provision of education services. Therefore, the Government of India should frame/ establish strong regulatory mechanism for controlling the entry/ operation of fake and sub-standard universities/institutions and it serves the purpose of protecting the higher education system.

6

Mode-wise Analysis of Trade in Higher Education Services

Opportunities and Challenges

Introduction

Education can be traded through four modes viz. Cross Border Supply, Consumption Abroad, Commercial Presence and Presence of Natural Persons.[1] These four modes of supply of education services are referred in General Agreement on Trade in Service (GATS) negotiation. The Mode II i.e. Consumption Abroad is an old phenomenon, and most seen popularized phenomenon of trade in higher education services throughout the world; under which students go to various countries for acquiring higher education, but in recent years it has taken its momentum under GATS and many countries are exploiting this opportunity through attracting overseas students to their education institutions. In this connection, an attempt has been made to analyze the mode-wise trade in education services in general and in particular Mode II i.e. Consumption Abroad in detail; further the mode-wise opportunities and challenges of higher education services has been analyzed.

A. Cross Border Supply

Under this mode, the service crosses a national border while the suppliers and consumers remain in different countries. Transmission of services can be made by voice, fax or data flow; by the dispatch of documents, discs, tapes and so on; or by mail or courier. The rapid development in Information and Communication Technology (ICT) Sector has led to considerable growth in the cross-border supply of services. It basically takes in two forms: Conventional distance education using print and audio visual material, and distance education using the Internet. Further, Distance Learning System does not consider national boundaries as important barriers to deliver of their programmes and most of the well-known distance education providers in the world have cross-border presence under existing regulatory framework.

If India made commitment to GATS in higher education including distance education, then domestic distance education providers should be ready for competing in international market particularly with overseas providers. The Most Favoured Nation (MFN) and National Treatment (NT) issues are very much concerned in this regard, as far as MFN agreement is concerned, India should treat all members of overseas distance education providers equally. For example, the IGNOU is providing progammes and study materials at favourable rates in Asian and African regions; this 'favoured treatment' should be extended to all members of WTO, elsewhere it would be treated as 'unfair' trade practice or it would be withdrawn.

The implication of 'National Treatment' is concerned, Government of India has to treat all overseas distance education providers equally as domestic providers are treated, which means it has to extend all supports being provided for domestic providers to overseas providers. The facilities like use of national broadcast facilities and receive sites and preferential rate structure for use of communication infrastructure etc. will be demanded by overseas providers.

In case of India, the Indira Gandhi National Open University (IGNOU) has prepared enough to compete with international level. It has successfully delivering its programmes abroad; it is providing academic and training programmes to overseas students in nearly 35 countries. The University promotes its academic programmes through the international cell by establishing bilateral and multi-lateral cooperation and exchanges. Currently, programmes are offered, in combination with face-to-face counselling support, in the places of African and Asian nations such as Abu Dhabi, Al Ayn, Doha, Dubai, Al Fujayrah, Kuwait, Sharjah, Sultanate of Oman (Muscat), Bahrain, Saudi Arabia, Seychelles, Mauritius, Maldives, Ethiopia, Liberia, Madagascar, Kenya, Namibia, Nigeria, Ghana, Sierra Leone, Zambia,

Zimbabwe, Tanzania, Myanmar, Vietnam, Singapore, Indonesia, Nepal, Sri Lanka, and Malaysia. Also, the University offers visiting fellowships to the academics and other categories of staff working in the open universities of Asia under the Inter-University Staff Exchange Scheme. The University hosts, supports and participates in national and international conferences to give impetus to research and encourage its academics. The University is participating in the Pan-African Project of Government of India as the main e-content provider for tele-education in 53 countries.

The Commonwealth of Learning has recognized the IGNOU as one of its centres of excellence. It also has the unique privilege of hosting the Secretariats of SAARC Consortium of Open Distance Learning (SACODiL) approved by Heads of Governments of SAARC Nations and Global Mega Universities Network (GMUNET) initially promoted by UNESCO.

IGNOU's remarkable success in collaborating with Open Universities in the SAARC region and International Organisations like Commonwealth of Learning, World Bank, World Intellectual Property Organisation, World Health Office, various Ministries, reputed Research Institutes and NGOs has helped it to develop niche market oriented areas such as Post Graduate Diploma in Environment and Sustainable Development, Intellectual Property Rights, Community Cardiology, Ophthalmology, Hospitality, Integrated Doctoral Programmes in Physics and Mathematics, HIV/AIDS, Disaster Management, Public Policy, Human Rights, Nautical Sciences, Power Distribution Management, Construction Workers, Rural Artisans, Motor Mechanics, Gandhi and Contemporary World etc. An important feature of IGNOU's course materials is its wide acceptability, authenticity and latest content at low cost and consequently IGNOU has competitive strength in marketing of its education programmes abroad. It is observed in Bhushan Subhanshu study that "IGNOU charges US $ 250 for its prestigious management course; whereas similar course from a developed country would cost at least ten times that of above charges" (Bhushan Subhanshu, 2004).

Even though, the IGNOU is marketing its education services successfully in most of the Asian countries, an assessment of the strength of IGNOU in marketing education abroad in comparison with international distance education providers is necessary for making offers. India can make requests to other countries to allow IGNOU to market its programme.

B. Consumption Abroad

Student mobility is currently the most prevalent form of trade in education services today. The phenomenon of student mobility is not new to India, earlier a chunk of students was moving abroad to acquire higher knowledge. In pre-independence period most of the Indians had to go European countries particularly England for higher studies, they have been going abroad for the last two centuries. In recent years, students are going abroad particularly US, UK, Canada, Australia, Germany etc., to acquire specialized knowledge (degrees), skills, and to improve their academic and technical capabilities. On the contrary to this earlier days, many Indian higher learning centres viz., Takshshila, Nalanda, Vikramshila, Nadia, Vallabhi, etc., attracted huge number of students and scholars from various parts of the world and in recent years, renowned institutions like IITs, IIMs, MAHE, IGNOU etc. are attracting huge foreign students. In this connection different aspects of foreign students' inflow and Indian students outflow i.e. year-wise, sex-wise, subject-wise, country-wise, continent-wise are presented and also explanation about the students gone abroad under different sources of financial assistance are presented and analyzed in this section in detail.

Comparison of Outflow of Indian Students and Inflow of Foreign Students

Basically, Consumption Abroad mode covers both International Students' inflow and Indian Students' outflow; to comprehend the position of these two aspects, the year-wise comparison of data has been presented in Table 6.1 and further the data has been analyzed. The facts provide the status of foreign students' inflow and Indian students' outflow from mid-80s (1986-87) to twenty first century (2001-02). It is observed that, the number of students going abroad is higher than the overseas students coming to India. During pre-WTO period, foreign students' inflow was high and increasing; however, fluctuating trend was observed in this period. During post-WTO period, foreign students coming to India was falling with fluctuating figures, at WTO establishment year i.e. 1995-96, the number of foreign students enrolled in Indian universities were highest comparing to rest of the years. During 1998-99 an unprecedented decline of foreign students' inflow was registered which is the lowest total in both pre-

and post-WTO periods; later an appreciable improvement has taken place in foreign students' inflow.

On the contrary, Indian students studying in foreign universities was less compared to foreign students studying in India during pre-WTO period, later the last two years of the period i.e. 1993-94 and 1994-95 registered lowest outflow of Indian students abroad for higher studies, which is all time low in both pre- and post-WTO period. During post-WTO period, Indian students' going abroad for higher studies is continuously increasing; a substantial increase has registered in between 1999-2000 to 2001-02. It has been observed that about 25 times increase in Indian students' outflow as on from 1995-96 to 2001-02. It clearly indicates that liberalization policies under WTO agreement paved the way for increase in students' outflow and on the other hand, aggressive advertising and marketing strategies of western

Table 6.1: Comparison of Indian Students Outflow Abroad and Foreign Students Inflow to India, 1986-87 to 2001-02

(*in Numbers*)

Year	*Foreign students studying in India*	*Indian students studying abroad*
1986-87	10820	3489
1990-91	12924	4861
1991-92	NA	6466
1992-93	12791	6499
1993-94	13723	2284
1994-95	11896	2983
1995-96	10087	3478
1996-97	5881	6426
1997-98	6701	6734
1998-99	5323	6918
1999-2000*	6988	51414
2000-01*	7791	61977
2001-02*	8145	87987
Pre-WTO Period, CGR for 1986-87 to 1994-95 (%)	1.19	-1.94
Post-WTO Period, CGR for 1995-96 to 2001-02 (%)	-3.50	71.34
Entire Period, CGR for 1986-87 to 2001-02 (%)	-1.88	24.01

Source: 1. Indian Students/Trainees going abroad (various series).
2. *Govt. of India, Selected Educational Statistics 2003-04, Ministry of Human Resource Development, New Delhi, p. 112.

Note: NA - Not Available.

countries (UK, USA, Australia, Germany etc.) are attracting more Indian students towards their destinations.

It has been observed that (Fig. 6.1), during Pre-WTO period the percentage of growth of foreign students' inflow is positive; at the same time Indian students' outflow was recorded negative growth rate because of slow down in number of Indian students going abroad. In Post-WTO period, foreign students' inflow to India is declining; therefore, the negative growth rate is registered, whereas Indian student's enrollment in foreign universities has increased continuously for the same period, hence highest positive growth rate of students outflow is registered.

As far as the entire period is concerned, foreign students' inflow is negative, which means total number of foreign students studying in Indian universities is declining as compared to previous years (1980s) and smaller number of foreign students are coming to India for higher studies. On the contrary, Indian students studying in foreign universities is increasing, therefore positive growth rate has registered for Indian students outflow, which clearly indicates that outgoing students number is increasing steadily much faster than inflow of

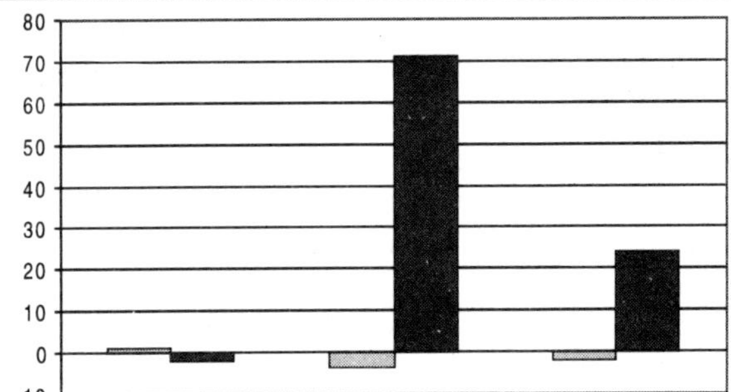

	Pre-WTO Period, (1986-87 to 1994-95) (%)	Post-WTO Period, (1995-96 to 2001-02) (%)	During Entire Period, (1986-87 to 2001-02) (%)
□ Foreign Students Inflow	1.19	-3.50	-1.88
■ Indian Students Outflow	-1.94	71.34	24.01

Source: Table 6.1

Fig. 6.1: Compound Growth Rates of Foreign Students Coming to India and Indian Students Going Abroad – A Comparative Picture of Pre- and Post-WTO Periods

foreign students. Hence, India has to redefine its higher education policy to accommodate the WTO agreements as well as to compete in global market and it has to implement aggressive advertising policy for attracting more foreign students.

Sex-wise Outflow of Indian Students Abroad

The data in Table 6.2 provides the details of annual outflow of India's male and female students, it is observed that, during Pre- and Post-WTO period the percentage of total outgoing female students for higher studies have increased; but fluctuating tendency was observed in between the both periods. On the other hand, in the beginning year of the Pre-WTO period i.e. 1986-87, a large portion of male students went abroad for higher studies, that portion of male students were little declined at the end of the period i.e. 1994-95. During Post-WTO period, marginal decline is observed in percentage of male students going abroad which is almost the same as to Pre-WTO period. However, Indian male students going abroad remained high as compared to female students in all the years of both Pre- and Post-WTO periods.

Figure 6.2 reveals that, in both Pre- and Post-WTO period growth of outgoing Indian female students is higher than male students; during Post-WTO period significant growth was registered as compared to former period. On the other hand, the growth of outgoing Indian male students was negative in Pre-WTO period, later on Post-WTO period growth rate is increased; however it is less than growth rate of outgoing female students. As far as the entire period is concerned; female students' percentage of growth was registered marginally higher than male students' percentage of growth, which depicts that annual growth of female students is marginally increasing towards foreign countries for higher studies in recent years. It clearly depicts that female students are now enjoying more liberty than earlier and equal opportunities are being provided for women in education, which may be one of the reasons to increase the outflow of female students to abroad, further it can be predicted that, attitude towards women is changing in modern society and women are empowering in all aspects of the life.

Outflow of Indian Students to Different Continents

The data presented in Table 6.3 shows that, the American continent

Table 6.2: Sex-wise Annual Outflow of Indian Students Abroad, 1986-87 to 1998-99

(in Numbers)

Year	*Male*	*Female*	*Total*
1986-87	3040 (87.13)	449 (12.87)	3489 (100.0)
1987-88	3690 (86.13)	594 (13.87)	4284 (100.0)
1990-91	4063 (83.58)	798 (16.42)	4861 (100.0)
1991-92	5579 (86.28)	887 (13.72)	6466 (100.0)
1992-93	5546 (85.34)	953 (14.66)	6499 (100.0)
1993-94	1887 (82.62)	397 (17.38)	2284 (100.0)
1994-95	2505 (83.98)	478 (16.02)	2983 (100.0)
1995-96	3001 (86.29)	477 (13.71)	3478 (100.0)
1996-97	5623 (87.50)	803 (12.50)	6426 (100.0)
1997-98	5673 (84.24)	1061 (15.76)	6734 (100.0)
1998-99	5806 (83.93)	1112 (16.07)	6918 (100.0)
Pre-WTO Period, CGR for 1986-87 to 1994-95 (%)	-2.39	0.79	-1.94
Post-WTO Period, CGR for 1995-96 to 1998-99 (%)	24.61	32.60	25.76
Entire Period, CGR for 1986-87 to 1998-99 (%)	5.54	7.85	5.87

Source: Indian Students/Trainees Going Abroad (various issues).

Note: 1. Data of 1985-86, 1988-89 and 1989-90 were not available.

2. Figures in parenthesis indicate the percentage share of the total.

has acquired a top position in attracting Indian students, however decreasing trend was observed in percentage of students. It is observed that during Pre-WTO period, beginning year i.e. 1986-87 major portion of outgoing students have chosen American continent as destination for their higher studies, at the end of the year i.e. 1994-95 of Pre-WTO period 29.65 per cent decline in outgoing students. During Post-WTO period also American continent remained in top position in attracting more students from India. Notwithstanding this, the share of Indian students to countries comprising American

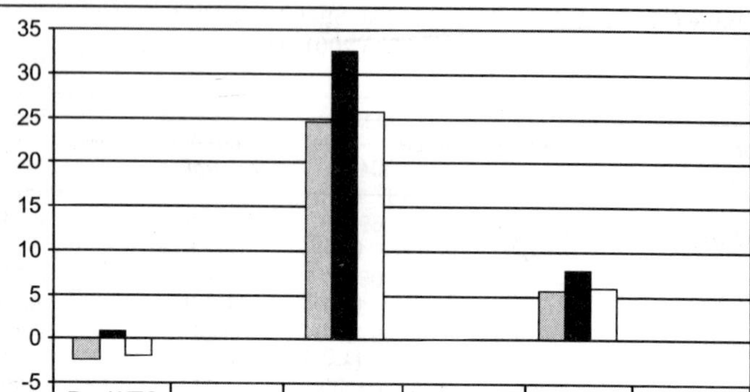

	Pre-WTO Period, (1986-87 to 1994-95)		Post-WTO Period, (1995-96 to 1998-99)		During Entire Period, (1986-87 to 1998-99)	
Male	-2.39		24.61		5.54	
Female	0.79		32.60		7.85	
Total	-1.94		25.76		5.87	

Source: Table 6.2.

Fig. 6.2: Compound Growth Rates of Sex-wise Number of Students Going Abroad - A Comparative Picture of Pre- and Post- WTO Periods

continent, by and large remains the largest amongst all continents of the world.

On the other hand, the percentage of annual outflow of Indian students to Oceania (Australia) continent is increasing. In Pre-WTO period, during 1986-87 it attracted very small per cent of Indian students, marginal increase in percentage of students is found at the end of the period i.e. 1994-95. Beginning of the WTO period i.e. 1995-96 increasing number of students went from India to Australia for higher learning, at the end of the period declining trend were observed.

Similar fluctuating trend of student outflow is observed in case of Europe also. The percentage of students studying in Europe increased during Pre-WTO period. In WTO regime i.e. 1995-96 total 21.22 per cent of Indian students were registered in European universities, which condensed to 11.03 per cent in 2001-02. The small percentage of Indian students are enrolling in Asian universities; and in case of African universities very negligible number of students

Table 6.3: Annual Outflow of Indian Students to Different Continents, 1986-87 to 2001-02

(in Numbers)

Year	*America*	*Europe*	*Asia*	*Oceania (Australia)*	*Others*	*Total*
1986-87	3113 (89.22)	292 (8.37)	24 (0.69)	31 (0.89)	29 (0.83)	3489 (100.0)
1987-88	3749 (87.51)	334 (7.80)	56 (1.31)	60 (1.40)	85 (1.98)	4284 (100.0)
1990-91	4310 (88.66)	314 (6.46)	51 (1.05)	132 (2.72)	54 (1.11)	4861 (100.0)
1991-92	5954 (92.08)	248 (3.84)	35 (0.54)	180 (2.78)	49 (0.76)	6466 (100.0)
1992-93	5787 (89.04)	240 (3.69)	39 (0.60)	376 (5.79)	57 (0.88)	6499 (100.0)
1993-94	1789 (78.33)	232 (10.16)	25 (1.09)	202 (8.84)	36 (1.58)	2284 (100.0)
1994-95	1777 (59.57)	570 (19.11)	42 (1.41)	552 (18.50)	42 (1.41)	2983 (100.0)
1995-96	1764 (50.72)	738 (21.22)	57 (1.64)	859 (24.70)	60 (1.73)	3478 (100.0)
1996-97	3022 (47.03)	1418 (22.07)	84 (1.31)	1714 (26.67)	188 (2.93)	6426 (100.0)
1997-98	2422 (35.97)	1637 (24.31)	146 (2.17)	2417 (35.89)	112 (1.66)	6734 (100.0)
1998-99	2579 (37.28)	1158 (16.74)	704 (10.18)	2357 (34.07)	120 (1.73)	6918 (100.0)
1999-2000*	39953 (77.71)	6274 (12.20)	408 (0.79)	4779 (9.30)	NA	51414 (100.0)
2000-01*	47411 (76.50)	6977 (11.26)	1039 (1.68)	6550 (10.57)	NA	61977 (100.0)
2001-02*	66844 (75.97)	9705 (11.03)	947 (1.08)	10491 (11.92)	NA	87987 (100.0)
Pre-WTO Period, CGR for 1986-87 to 1994-95 (%)	-6.77	8.72	7.25	43.33	4.74	-1.94
Post-WTO Period, CGR for 1995-96 to 2001-02 (%)	83.27	53.63	59.74	51.75	25.99**	71.34
Entire Period, CGR for 1986-87 to 2001-02 (%)	22.69	26.31	27.76	47.45	12.56***	24.01

Source: 1. Indian Students/Trainees Going Abroad (various issues).
2. * Government of India, Selected Educational Statistics 2003-04, Ministry of Human Resource Development, p.112.

Notes:
1. Data of 1988-89 &1989-90 were not available.
2. Figures in parenthesis indicate the percentage share for different continents.
3. NA - Not Available.
4. **Compound Growth Rate calculated for 1995-96 to 1998-99.
5. *** Compound Growth Rate calculated for 1986-87 to 1998-99.

were registered, it is clear that countries of Asian and African continents receive very lesser number of Indian students as compared to America, Oceania and Europe.

The above analysis distinctively indicates that the three continents viz. America, Europe and Oceania put together accounts highest percentage of the Indian students in Pre- and Post-WTO periods, leaving thereby, a very small fraction of the students to remaining continents viz. Asia and Africa. Secondly, the American continent has dominated in absorbing the large number of Indian students, followed by Oceania and Europe.

A comparative picture of students outflow depicts that, in pre-WTO period, Oceania (Australia) continent has registered highest percentage of growth rate of Indian students outflow compared to other continents, followed by Europe, which registered second highest

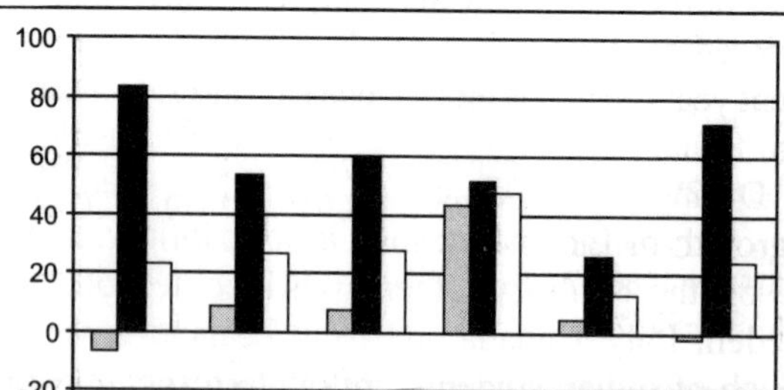

	America	Europe	Asia	Oceania	Others	Total
Pre-WTO Period (1986-87 to 1994-95) (%)	-6.77	8.72	7.25	43.33	4.74	-1.94
Post-WTO Period (1995-96 to 2001-02) (%)	83.27	53.63	59.74	51.75	25.99	71.34
During entire Period (1986-87 to 2001-02) (%)	22.69	26.31	27.76	47.45	12.56	24.01

Source: Table 6.3.

Fig. 6.3: Compound Growth Rates of Annual Outflow of Indian Students to different Continents - A Comparative Picture of Pre- and Post- WTO Periods

growth rate, but American continent registered a negative growth rate and Asia placed on third position. During post-WTO period, significant growth of Indian students outflow has been registered for American continent, followed by Asia, Europe and Australia. As Entire period is concerned, Australia recorded highest growth, followed by Asia, Europe and America.

The above analysis concludes that, Australia and European continents are emerging in international education market; further they are providing stiff competition to America in attracting overseas students. Through adopting aggressive advertising and marketing strategies Australian, European and American universities are succeeding in attracting more Indian students towards their educational institutions. Current WTO regime is positively contributing for Australian, European and American continents, since they recorded higher growth of Indian students' inflow into their universities.

Outflow of Indian Students to Different Countries

The data presented in Table 6.4 shows that, the majority of the students has chosen high income countries as their favoured destination in both pre- and post-WTO periods; as for instance, in the year 2001-02 major portion of Indian students were studying in U.S.A. universities, followed by Australia and U.K., Germany and New Zealand and in recent years Switzerland, France etc., are also attracting more students from India.

During pre-WTO period, Australia registered higher percentage of growth of Indian students' inflow, followed by Switzerland, UK and on the contrary, other high income countries such as USA, Sweden, Italy, Canada and New Zealand have registered negative growth of Indian students' inflow to respective countries. It clearly indicates that, only few developed countries have attracted more Indian students and others failed in attracting Indian students.

Under current WTO regime, high income countries are exploiting the opportunities created by the liberalization policies, they are attracting more Indian students through the well thought out strategies, and consequently higher growth rate is registered. Australia, Switzerland, UK, USA, Sweden registered higher growth of Indian students inflow; and countries like Italy, France and New Zealand have registered significantly highest growth among others.

It is being stated that USA, UK and Australia considered education as an important export commodity and consequently they are earning huge amount of foreign exchange from overseas students. It has been observed from the study conducted by Ahmad Nighat (2004) that Foreign students contribute about US $ 11 billion to the US economy, over AUS $ 4.2 billion to the Australian economy annually, now it represents Australia's eighth largest export sector and the Britain's economy earning £ 11 billion annually from export of education services.

Now Australia has started marketing of its educational services with competitive spirit in international market to attract overseas students, further countries such as Germany, New Zealand and France are emerging as key players in international higher education market; more students are choosing these nations as destination for their higher studies under current WTO period.

The important observation drawn from Table 6.4 is that Western Countries particularly USA, Australia, UK, Germany, New Zealand, France and Switzerland have adopted aggressive marketing strategies to attract overseas students in particular Indian students. Also, a wide variety of Asian countries are seeking to attract Indian students. Malaysia is already successful in attracting a variety of international students from South East Asia and India; probably it has already over 1,00,000 international students enrolled on its programmes.

Under WTO regime, the middle income countries are showing keen interest in attracting more Indian students to their countries; it clearly indicates that, the middle income countries viz. Malaysia, Thailand, Philippines and Hungary have prepared themselves for exploiting the opportunities in education sector; which are created by WTO agreements.

State-wise Outflow of Indian Students to Abroad

The data presented in Table 6.5 shows that, among the total outgoing students of the country, middle income states accounts highest i.e. more than 50 per cent in all the referred years, particularly states like Tamil Nadu, Andhra Pradesh and Karnataka are sending more students abroad, even though these states have good number of higher education institutions in the country.

In the year 1991 nearly 57.59 per cent of students went to foreign universities from middle income category states of the country; but

Table 6.4: Selected Country-wise Annual Outflow of Indian Students going Abroad, 1986-87 to 2001-02

(in Numbers)

Country	1986-87	1987-88	1990-91	1991-92	1993-94	1994-95	1996-97	1997-98	1998-99	1999-2000	2000-01	2001-02	Pre-WTO Period, CGR for 1986-87 to 1994-95 (%)	Post-WTO Period, CGR for 1996-97 to 2001-02 (%)	Entire Period, CGR for 1986-87 to 2001-02 (%)
HIGH INCOME ECONOMIES															
U.S.A.	2986	3686	4234	5883	1744	1729	2913	2374	2525	39084	47411	66836	-6.60	87.13	23.03
U.K.	183	202	227	193	99	262	693	961	1039	3962	4302	6016	4.59	54.07	26.22
France	20	24	19	11	20	23	4	11	15	185	239	309	1.76	138.55	20.02
Germany	NA	NA	NA	11	5	11	11	14	14	1262	1412	2196	--	188.43	69.83*
Australia	21	45	126	138	201	548	1712	2409	2345	4578	6195	9539	50.34	40.99	50.37
Belgium	4	7	1	9	1	4	35	8	4	113	129	137	0.00	31.38	26.56
Italy	14	14	7	4	3	5	1	NA	1	67	115	138	-12.08	167.90	16.48
Netherlands	1	12	3	5	5	7	5	9	10	38	49	53	27.54	60.35	30.30
New Zealand	10	15	6	7	1	4	1	8	5	201	355	953	-10.82	294.29	35.50
Spain	2	1	1	NA	NA	2	3	2	1	62	46	53	0.00	77.60	24.42
Sweden	6	13	11	4	NA	1	6	2	8	85	97	122	-20.07	82.66	22.24
Switzerland	10	NA	NA	NA	NA	79	82	39	50	93	120	162	29.48	14.59	20.40
Canada	127	63	76	71	44	48	109	48	54	867	NA	NA	-11.45	--	15.92**
China	0	1	12	2	4	4	2	7	1	NA	NA	NA	--	--	--
U.S.S.R. (CIR)	8	22	35	34	98	166	572	576	594	NA	NA	NA	46.09	--	43.18***

(Contd.)

Table 6.4: (*Contd.*)

Country	1986-87	1987-88	1990-91	1991-92	1993-94	1994-95	1996-97	1997-98	1998-99	1999-2000	2000-01	2001-02	Pre-WTO Period, CGR for 1986-87 to 1994-95 (%)	Post-WTO Period, CGR for 1996-97 to 2001-02 (%)	Entire Period, CGR for 1986-87 to 2001-02 (%)
MIDDLE INCOME ECONOMIES															
Malaysia	0	3	1	NA	1	NA	2	5	3	91	714	497	--	201.35	44.05****
Thailand	NA	7	7	3	4	5	3	10	3	NA	56	104	--	103.23	21.26****
Philippines	13	11	9	9	3	13	55	75	58	83	66	80	0.00	7.78	12.88
Hungary	2	0	1	NA	NA	2	NA	2	4	0	60	64	0.00	--	25.99
LOW INCOME ECONOMIES															
Bangladesh	0	0	0	1	NA	1	1	7	2	NA	NA	NA	--	--	--
Indonesia	0	0	0	0	0	0	0	3	4	1	1	1	--	--	--

Source: 1. Indian Students/Trainees Going Abroad (various issues).

2. Government of India, Selected Educational Statistics 2003-04, Ministry of Human Resource Development, New Delhi, p.112.

Notes: 1. Data of 1988-89 &1989-90, 1992-93, 1995-96 were not available.

2. NA - Not Available.

3. Classification of countries has been made on the bases of World Bank Report 2000.

4. *Compound growth rate calculated for 1991-92 to 2001-02, **CGR calculated for 1986-87 to 1999-2000, ***CGR calculated for 1986-87 to 1998-99, ****CGR calculated for 1987-88 to 2001-02.

during 1998 declined trend appeared in outgoing students' percentage i.e. 51.48 per cent. The states belonging to high income category stands at second position in total outgoing students. During 1991 nearly 24.11 per cent students went abroad from all states of high income category, which declined to 11.76 per cent in the year 1998. In this category Maharashtra, Punjab and Haryana states had major share.

Whereas the Low Income states are placed at third position, since small percentage of students from low income states went to foreign universities. Earlier i.e. in 1991 just 5.18 per cent students went abroad; but in current WTO period it is increased to 11.08 per cent in 1998. In this group, Bihar, Madhya Pradesh and Uttar Pradesh accounts highest percentage since 1991. In case of Delhi more students are going foreign universities for higher education; in 1991 it was 11.52 per cent of total outflow of students, which increased to 20.74 per cent in the year 1998.

As far as Special Category States and Union Territories are concerned, the trend is very meagre which accounts less than one per cent of total outgoing students, except Assam, J&K and Chandigarh. It indicates that, students belonging to these places are either facing dearth of information regarding foreign studies and facilities or lesser interested towards higher studies, in particularly foreign higher studies.

During pre-WTO period, the all Low Income states had positive growth rate in students' outflow; on the contrary during post-WTO period except Orissa other states have registered negative growth. But no uniform growth rate was found in case of both high income and middle income states in this respect. But an interesting thing is that, middle income states have registered highest percentage of outgoing students during the entire period 1990-1998 (see, Fig. 6.4).

Students Going Abroad Under Different Financial Sources

The data presented in Table 6.6 shows that, the majority of students who went abroad for higher studies met out their expenses from the unidentified sources; closely followed by self-financing source. During the beginning year i.e. 1986-87 of pre-WTO period, 54.49 per cent of students went abroad through unidentified sources; further it marginally increased at the end of the period i.e. in 1994-95, next to this self-financed source stands at second position where students

Table 6.5: State-wise Percentage of Students Going Abroad, 1991 to 1998

States/UTs	*1991*	*1992*	*1993*	*1994*	*1995*	*1996*	*1997*	*1998*	*Pre-WTO Period, CGR for 1991 to 1994 (%)*	*Post-WTO Period, CGR for 1995 to 1998 (%)*	*Entire Period, CGR for 1991 to 1998 (%)*
HIGH INCOME STATES											
Gujarat	2.30	3.12	4.55	2.72	1.21	0.42	0.55	0.62	5.75	-19.98	-17.08
Haryana	0.73	0.58	0.92	1.17	1.87	1.54	1.95	2.16	17.03	4.92	16.76
Maharashtra	19.35	14.85	13.00	8.45	6.30	2.83	6.18	6.14	-24.13	-0.85	-15.12
Punjab	1.58	0.94	1.93	1.71	1.84	2.94	2.76	2.51	2.67	10.91	6.84
Goa	0.15	0.08	0.00	0.34	0.78	0.40	0.48	0.33	31.36	-24.93	11.92
MIDDLE INCOME STATES											
Andhra Pradesh	30.40	30.74	23.25	16.63	2.19	19.87	6.44	8.51	-18.22	57.22	-16.63
Karnataka	7.87	11.74	10.73	9.02	7.76	7.95	12.19	10.65	4.65	11.13	4.42
Kerala	2.35	1.48	1.77	3.42	4.69	3.97	2.94	3.22	13.32	-11.78	4.60
Tamil Nadu	12.81	17.36	16.86	9.29	20.81	18.75	21.36	19.62	-10.16	-1.94	6.28
West Bengal	4.16	5.39	5.21	12.34	10.03	7.37	10.46	9.48	43.68	-1.86	12.49
LOW INCOME STATES											
Bihar	0.56	0.63	1.09	6.74	7.70	8.26	6.36	6.44	129.17	-5.78	41.75
Madhya Pradesh	1.98	0.26	1.62	2.51	2.01	1.01	0.92	1.70	8.23	-5.43	-2.15
Orissa	0.40	0.08	0.13	0.44	0.23	0.53	0.76	0.36	3.23	16.11	-1.49
Rajasthan	0.48	0.54	0.22	0.54	1.43	1.09	0.67	0.60	4.00	-25.14	3.24
Uttar Pradesh	1.76	1.71	1.80	4.96	5.52	2.19	2.78	2.70	41.25	-21.21	6.30

(*Contd.*)

Table 6.5: (*Contd.*)

States/UTs	*1991*	*1992*	*1993*	*1994*	*1995*	*1996*	*1997*	*1998*	*Pre-WTO Period, CGR for 1991 to 1994 (%)*	*Post-WTO Period, CGR for 1995 to 1998 (%)*	*Entire Period, CGR for 1991 to 1998 (%)*
SPECIAL CATEGORY STATES											
Arunachal Pradesh	—	0.01	—	0.03	—	0.03	0.03	0.04	—	—	—
Assam	0.48	0.28	0.26	0.57	1.18	0.51	0.64	0.79	5.90	-12.52	7.38
Himachal Pradesh	0.05	0.01		0.07	0.12	0.11	0.09	0.07	11.87	-16.45	4.92
Jammu & Kashmir	0.26	0.20	0.44	0.30	0.37	0.44	0.43	1.27	4.89	50.85	25.43
Manipur	0.01	0.03	—	0.03	0.03	0.02	0.01	0.08	44.22	38.67	34.59
Meghalaya	0.14	0.01	0.18	0.17	0.12	0.08	0.22	0.31	6.69	37.21	12.03
Mizoram	0.01	—	—	0.13	0.12	0.08	0.09	0.02	135.13	-44.97	10.41
Nagaland	—	—	—	0.13	0.09	0.02	0.03	0.04	—	-23.69	—
Sikkim	0.01	0.03	—	0.03	0.03	0.02	0.01	0.05	44.22	18.56	25.85
Tripura	—	—	—	—	0.03	—	0.01	0.14	—	67.11	—
UNION TERRITORIES											
A & N Islands	0.01	0.01	—	—	—	—	0.00	—	-100.00	—	-100.00
Chandigarh	0.60	0.32	2.23	1.11	1.66	0.62	1.47	1.41	22.76	-5.30	12.98
D & N Haveli	—	—	—	—	—	0.47	0.01	—	—	—	—
Delhi	11.52	9.56	14.14	17.1	21.8	18.5	20.15	20.74	13.98	-1.59	8.76
Pondicherry	—	0.03	—	0.10	0.12	0.02	0.01	—	—	-100.00	—
INDIA	100.0	100.0	100.0	100.0	100.0	100.0	100.0	100.0			

Source: Indian Students/Trainees Going Abroad 1998-99, Ministry of Human Resource Development, Govt. of India, p. 5.

Note: 1. *Classification of States has been made on the bases of twelfth Finance Commission Report.

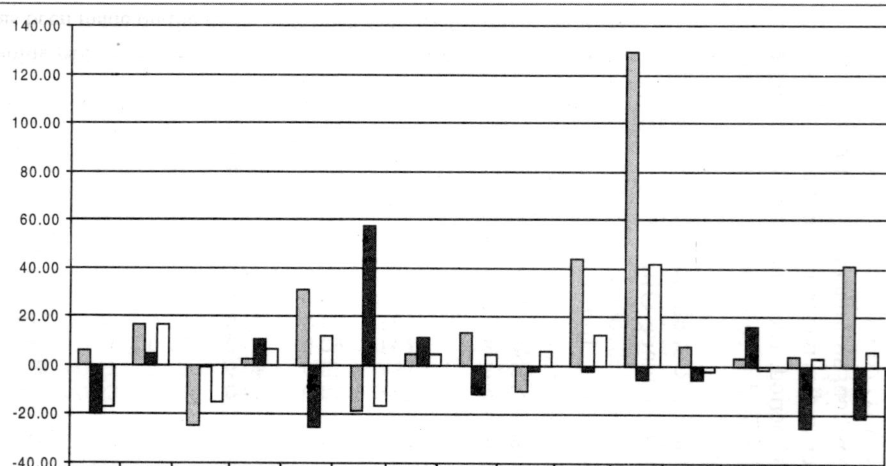

	High Income States					Middle Income States					Low Income States				
	Guj	Har	Mah	Pun	Goa	A P	Kar	Ker	T N	W B	Bih	M P	Ori	Raj	U P
Pre-WTO Period (1991 to 1994) (%)	5.75	17.03	-24.13	2.67	31.36	-18.22	4.65	13.32	-10.16	43.68	129.1	8.23	3.23	4.00	41.25
Post-WTO Period (1995 to 1998) (%)	-20	4.92	-0.85	10.91	-24.9	57.22	11.13	-11.8	-1.94	-1.86	-5.78	-5.43	16.11	-25.1	-21.2
During Entire Period (1991 to 1998) (%)	-17.1	16.76	-15.1	6.84	11.92	-16.6	4.42	4.60	6.28	12.49	41.75	-2.15	-1.49	3.24	6.30

Source: Table 6.5.

Fig. 6.4: Compound Growth Rates for State-wise Percentage of Students Going Abroad - A Comparative Picture of Pre- and Post-WTO Periods

were pursuing higher education in foreign universities on their own expenses. During the post-WTO period also, these two sources have maintained their earlier position; still major portion of the students are going abroad for higher studies under unidentified sources which is higher than the pre-WTO period. The remaining sources of finance were not significantly influenced or contributed on students' outflow for pursuing higher studies.

In pre-WTO period, the CGR of all financial sources registered negative growth except Assistance Offered by Foreign Units/ Institutions source; even unidentified source and Self-financing source also registered negative growth. But during post-WTO period, significant growth is registered for sources like Central/Foreign Govt. Scholarships; Unidentified source, Self-financing source. As the entire period is considered, except three sources viz. Assistance Offered by Foreign Units/Institutions source, unidentified source and Self-financing source registered negative growth. It indicates that domestic and foreign government, education institutions, agencies are providing more financial facilities to students for higher studies and the signing of Memorandum of Understanding (MoU) is increasing during post-WTO period.

Selected Country-wise Indian Students for Foreign Scholarships

The data presented in Table 6.7 shows that, during 2004-05 and 2005-06 almost same per cent of foreign scholarships have been utilized by the Indian students i.e. 42 per cent, however the utilization of foreign scholarships are concerned the year 2005-06 is better than 2004-05.

During 2004-05 about 42 per cent of total nominated foreign scholarships were utilized which is very less in size; Japan followed by Slovak and Iran stood at top position among the utilized foreign scholarships by Indian students; the remaining foreign countries scholarships were utilized at less than 50 per cent. On the other hand, during 2005-06 Israel followed by Slovak, Japan, Mexico, Czech and China stand at top position among the utilized foreign scholarships by Indian students; the remaining foreign countries scholarships were utilized at less than 50 per cent. It indicates that little improvement has taken place in the utilization of foreign scholarships as compared to 2004-05 (*see* Fig. 6.6).

Table 6.6: Financial Assistance, 1986-87 to 2001-02

(in Numbers)

Source	*1986-87*	*1987-88*	*1990-91*	*1991-92*	*1992-93*	*1993-94*	*1994-95*	*1995-96*	*1996-97*	*1997-98*	*1998-99*	*Pre-WTO Period, CGR for 1986-87 to 1994-95 (%)*	*Post WTO Period, CGR for 1995-96 to 1998-99 (%)*	*Entire Period CGR f 1986-8 to 199 99 (%*
Central/Foreign Govt. Scholarships	47* (1.35)	92* (2.15)	25* (0.51)	56 (0.87)	147 (2.26)	35 (1.53)	5 (0.17)	17 (0.49)	125 (1.95)	124 (1.84)	413 (5.97)	-24.43	189.62	19.85
State Government funds	—	—	—	5 (0.08)	0 (0.00)	0 (0.00)	1 (0.03)	1 (0.03)	0 (0.00)	0 (0.00)	0 (0.00)	-41.52**	-100.00	-100.00
Commonwealth Scholarships	—	—	—	5 (0.08)	0 (0.00)	0 (0.00)	1 (0.03)	0 (0.00)	1 (0.02)	1 (0.01)	0 (0.00)	-41.52**	—	-100.00
Scholarship offered by Foreign Units/University	220 (6.31)	82 (1.91)	18 (0.37)	14 (0.22)	7 (0.11)	47 (2.06)	212 (7.11)	59 (1.70)	9 (0.14)	9 (0.13)	70 (1.01)	-0.46	5.86	-9.10
Assistance offered by Foreign Units/Institution	—	—	—	14 (0.22)	0 (0.00)	34 (1.49)	17 (0.57)	15 (0.43)	3 (0.05)	29 (0.43)	8 (0.12)	6.69**	-18.90	-7.68**
Free-ship offered by Foreign University/Institute	—	—	—	1 (0.02)	0 (0.00)	7 (0.31)	0 (0.00)	0 (0.00)	2 (0.03)	2 (0.03)	0 (0.00)	-100.00**	—	-100.00
Self-financing (Partly)	84 (2.41)	115 (2.68)	47 (0.97)	62 (0.96)	108 (1.66)	17 (0.74)	45 (1.51)	48 (1.38)	44 (0.68)	90 (1.34)	64 (0.93)	-7.51	10.06	-2.24
Self-financing (Fully)	1237 (35.45)	1515 (35.36)	676 (13.91)	1231 (19.04)	1357 (20.88)	726 (31.79)	1011 (33.89)	1212 (34.85)	1917 (29.83)	1544 (22.93)	1635 (23.63)	-2.49	10.49	2.35
Expenses met by Indian Company	—	—	—	3 (0.05)	26 (0.40)	7 (0.31)	0 (0.00)	4 (0.12)	3 (0.05)	4 (0.06)	1 (0.01)	-100.00**	-37.00	-14.52*

(Contd.)

Table 6.6: *(Contd.)*

Source	1986-87	1987-88	1990-91	1991-92	1992-93	1993-94	1994-95	1995-96	1996-97	1997-98	1998-99	Pre-WTO Period, CGR for 1986-87 to 1994-95 (%)	Post WTO Period, CGR for 1995-96 to 1998-99 (%)	Entire Period, CGR for 1986-87 to 1998-99 (%)
Expenses met by Foreign Company	—	—	—	0 (0.00)	0 (0.00)	0 (0.00)	0 (0.00)	5 (0.14)	7 (0.11)	1 (0.01)	0 (0.00)	—	-100.00	—
Scholarship offered by All Indian Universities	—	—	—	0 (0.00)	0 (0.00)	0 (0.00)	10 (0.34)	2 (0.06)	3 (0.05)	1 (0.01)	1 (0.01)	—	-20.63	—
Others (Not specified)	1901 (54.49)	2480 (57.89)	4095 (84.24)	5075 (78.49)	4854 (74.69)	1411 (61.78)	1681 (56.35)	2115 (60.81)	4312 (67.10)	4929 (73.20)	4726 (68.31)	-1.53	30.74	7.88
Total	3489 (100)	4284 (100)	4861 (100)	6466 (100)	6499 (100)	2284 (100)	2983 (100)	3478 (100)	6426 (100)	6734 (100)	6918 (100)	-1.94	25.76	5.87

Source: Indian Students/Trainees Going Abroad (various issues)

Note: 1. Data of 1988-89 &1989-90, were not available.

2. Figures in parenthesis indicate the percentage share of the total.
3. *Figures includes Central/Foreign & State govt. funds/Scholarships
4. **Compound Growth Rate Calculated for 1991-92 to 1994-95.
5. *** Compound Growth Rate Calculated for 1991-92 to 1998-99.
6. From 1986-87 to 1990-91, Students Statistical Break-up was not available for the Financial Sources viz. Commonwealth Scholarships; Assistance Offered by Foreign Units/Institution, Free-ship offered by Foreign University/Institute, Expenses met by Indian & Foreign Companies and Scholarship offered by All Indian Universities.

Table 6.7: Selected Country-wise Number of Students for Foreign Scholarship, 2004-05 and 2005-06

Country	*2004-05*			*2005-06*		
	Nominated	*Utilized*	*%age Utilized*	*Nominated*	*Utilized (Up to Dec. 2005)*	*Percentage Utilized*
Japan	37	30	81.08	32	28	87.50
China	23	11	47.83	26	13	50.00
Israel	9	2	22.22	6	6	100.00
Mexico	4	—	0.00	4	3	75.00
Slovak	3	2	66.67	2	2	100.00
Czech	3	1	33.33	3	2	66.67
Iran	8	5	62.50	—	—	—
U.K.	57	22	38.60	55	19	34.55
Canada	35	6	17.14	21	7	33.33
Belgium	8	3	37.50	8	1	12.50
Italy	31	14	45.16	48	9	18.75
Portugal	6	1	16.67	7	1	14.29
Norway	10	3	30.00	6	2	33.33
Greece	4	—	0.00	1	—	0.00
Grand Total	238	100	42.02	219	93	42.47

Source: Ministry of Human Resource Development, Government of India, 2005.

Distribution of Students by Fields of Studies

The data presented in Table 6.8 shows that, during pre-WTO period, most of the Indian students went abroad for studying Engineering and Architect courses, whereas Science stood at second position in attracting Indian students; it means that higher percentage of students opted Science course next to Engineering and Architect courses. Beginning of the period about 1/5th portion of total students opted Science; later on at the end of the pre-WTO period it reduced to 1/10 of the total student population of going abroad for choosing the Science subject.

During post-WTO period, Commerce, Business Administration/ Business Management fields are emerged as most demanding one for higher studies, as a result of this the respective field of study stands at first position in attracting Indian students in said period. At the same time, steep decline is observed in selecting the courses viz. Engineering and Architect; Science courses compared to pre-WTO

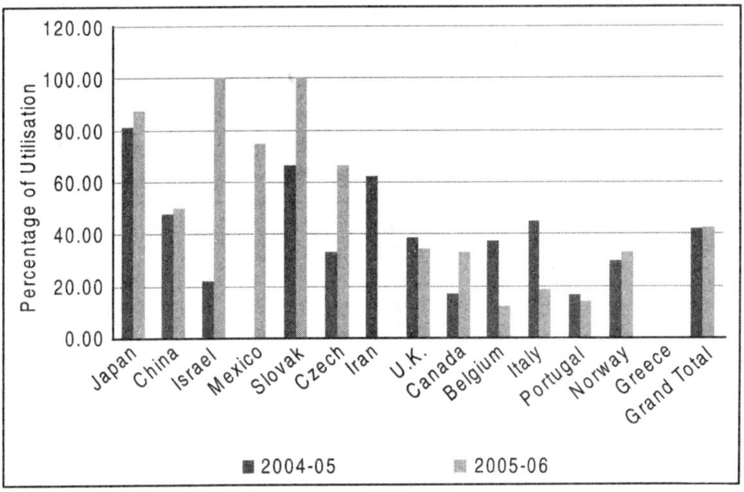

Source: Table 6.7.

Fig. 6.5: Country-wise comparison of Indian students for Foreign Scholarship

period. The number of students choosing Medicine, Pharmacy and Veterinary Science fields in pre-WTO period was small, but during post-WTO period it marginally increased. But for other courses, a very small number of students are going abroad for pursue subjects like Education, Nursing, Fine Arts and Library Science etc.

The conclusion is drawn from the available data of Table 6.8 that largest number of students are going abroad for studying courses like engineering and architect, science, technology & industry and commerce, business administration/management courses during the all years, where these three field of studies absorbing around 60 to 70 per cent of Indian students. However, no specific trend is observed in any field of study, since there is fluctuating trend observed throughout the entire period. The employment market is demanding the graduates of commerce, business administration and management; hence the demand for respective courses is increasing within and outside the country; due to the increasing opportunities in these fields students are choosing said courses for their higher studies on top priorities.

It is revealed from Figure 6.7 that, during pre-WTO period, except commerce, business administration/business management, agriculture and forestry, law and fine art, remaining subjects have shown negative

Table 6.8: Distribution of Indian Students by Fields of Studies, 1986-87 to 1997-98

Fields of Study	*1986-87*	*1987-88*	*1990-91*	*1991-92*	*1992-93*	*1993-94*	*1994-95*	*1995-96*	*1996-97*	*1997-98*	*1998-99*	*Pre-WTO Period, CGR for 1986-87 to 1994-95 (%)*	*Post-WTO Period, CGR for 1995-96 to 1998-99 (%)*	*Entire Period, CGR for 1986-87 to 1998-99 (%)*
Engineering & Architect	1179	1487	1838	2390	2460	709	792	703	1473	1014	1156	-4.85	18.03	-0.16
	(33.79)	(34.71)	(37.81)	(36.96)	(37.85)	(31.04)	(26.55)	(20.21)	(22.92)	(15.06)	(16.71)			
Science	722	727	1097	1384	1447	575	340	387	631	789	923	-8.98	33.61	2.07
	(20.69)	(16.97)	(22.57)	(21.40)	(22.26)	(25.18)	(11.40)	(11.13)	(9.82)	(11.72)	(13.34)			
Education	14	43	2	3	1	NA	2	9	5	33	5	-21.59	-17.79	-8.22
	(0.40)	(1.00)	(0.04)	(0.05)	(0.02)		(0.07)	(0.26)	(0.08)	(0.49)	(0.07)			
Technology & Industry	177	147	122	121	115	43	141	98	381	325	540	-2.80	76.63	9.74
	(5.07)	(3.43)	(2.51)	(1.87)	(1.77)	(1.88)	(4.73)	(2.82)	(5.93)	(4.83)	(7.81)			
Commerce, Business Adm., Business Management	529	109	609	946	795	341	646	957	1777	2592	2342	2.53	34.76	13.20
	(15.16)	(2.54)	(12.53)	(14.63)	(12.23)	(14.93)	(21.66)	(27.52)	(27.65)	(38.49)	(33.85)			
Arts	156	135	190	204	191	130	111	177	235	302	353	-4.16	25.87	7.04
	(4.47)	(3.15)	(3.91)	(3.15)	(2.94)	(5.69)	(3.72)	(5.09)	(3.66)	(4.48)	(5.10)			
Agriculture & Forestry	8	43	247	94	66	12	16	15	80	11	6	9.05	-26.32	-2.37
	(0.23)	(1.00)	(5.08)	(1.45)	(1.02)	(0.53)	(0.54)	(0.43)	(1.24)	(0.16)	(0.09)			
Medicine, Pharmacy & Veterinary Science	110	182	56	350	449	85	327	370	907	607	646	14.59	20.41	15.90
	(3.15)	(4.25)	(1.15)	(5.41)	(6.91)	(3.72)	(10.96)	(10.64)	(14.11)	(9.01)	(9.34)			
Law	14	13	18	26	21	9	18	23	43	55	66	3.19	42.10	13.79
	(0.40)	(0.30)	(0.37)	(0.40)	(0.32)	(0.39)	(0.60)	(0.66)	(0.67)	(0.82)	(0.95)			
Bank/Banking Institution	—	—	4	14	6	9	2	25	38	15	35	-15.91*	11.87	31.14**
			(0.08)	(0.22)	(0.09)	(0.39)	(0.07)	(0.72)	(0.59)	(0.22)	(0.51)			

(Contd.)

Table 6.8: (*Contd.*)

Fields of Study	*1986-87*	*1987-88*	*1990-91*	*1991-92*	*1992-93*	*1993-94*	*1994-95*	*1995-96*	*1996-97*	*1997-98*	*1998-99*	*Pre-WTO Period, CGR for 1986-87 to 1994-95 (%)*	*Post-WTO Period, CGR for 1995-96 to 1998-99 (%)*	*Entire Period, CGR for 1986-87 to 1998-99 (%)*
Nursing	—	—	2	NA	2	NA	NA	1	1	4	1	—	0.00	-8.30**
			(0.04)		(0.03)			(0.03)	(0.02)	(0.06)	(0.01)			
Fine Arts	—	—	29	30	69	NA	42	39	69	62	46	9.70*	5.66	5.94**
			(0.60)	(0.46)	(1.06)	.	(1.41)	(1.12)	(1.07)	(0.92)	(0.66)			
Library Science	—	—	NA	1	0	NA	3	1	7	1	NA	—	—	—
				(0.02)			(0.10)	(0.03)	(0.11)	(0.01)				
Others	580	1398	647	904	877	371	543	673	779	924	799	-0.82	5.89	2.71
	(16.62)	(32.63)	(13.31)	(13.98)	(13.49)	(16.24)	(18.20)	(19.35)	(12.12)	(13.72)	(11.55)			
Total	3489	4284	4861	6466	6499	2284	2983	3478	6426	6734	6918	-1.94	25.76	5.87
	(100)	(100)	(100)	(100)	(100)	(100)	(100)	(100)	(100)	(100)	(100)			

Source: Indian Students/Trainees Going Abroad (various issues).

Note:
1. Data of 1988-89 &1989-90, were not available.
2. Figures in parenthesis indicate the percentage share of the total.
3. *Compound Growth Rate Calculated for 1990-91 to 1994-95.
4. **Compound Growth Rate Calculated for 1990-91 to 1998-99.
5. During 1986-87 &1987-88 distribution of Students by field of Studies was not available for Banking Institution, Nursing, Fine Arts and Library Science.

growth. But in post-WTO period, only agriculture and forestry and education registered negative growth. Whereas Technology and Industry registered highest per cent growth rate among other subjects in attracting Indian students as fields for higher studies in abroad; while commerce, business administration/business management fields registered third highest per cent growth.

Continent-wise Inflow of International Students

The data presented in Table 6.9 reveals that, major portion of international students are coming to India from countries of Asian continent. Compared to pre-WTO period there is increase in the percentage of students coming to India for higher studies from Asian continent during post-WTO period; at the end of the post-WTO period i.e. 2004-05 about 3/4th of total international students were coming from Asian countries. Notwithstanding this, the share of Asian continent countries students to India, by and large, remains the largest among all continents of the world.

Students coming from countries of Africa continent have fallen; during pre-WTO period, about ½ portion of students belonging to Africa were studying which almost remained same on said period. In case of post-WTO period steep decline in the international students' enrollment in Indian universities is observed.

Students from American continent coming to India for pursuing higher studies is slightly increasing with fluctuating percentage in both pre- and post-WTO periods; however very small percentage of students are coming from American continent for higher studies. In case of European continent also small percentage of students were coming to India for higher studies; there is slight decline in the percentage of students during post-WTO period as compared to pre-WTO period. The students from Oceania (Australia) continent in India are very negligible in both pre- and post-WTO periods; which are less than 1.00 per cent of international students. In this way, India receives very small number of students from Australian continent followed by American continent and since beginning of pre-WTO period to end of the post-WTO period.

Important observations are being drawn from the above analysis: Students belonging to developing countries of Asian and African continents are representing major portion of overseas students in India. The inflow of students from Asia is more because of similar climatic

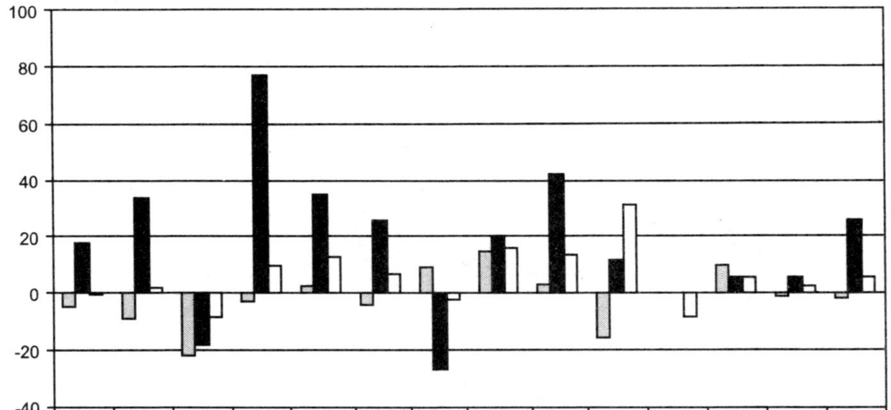

	Engg. & Tech.	Sci.	Educ.	Tech & Ind.	Comm. Busi.	Arts	Agri. & Fore.	Med., Pharm.	Law	Bank. Serv.	Nur-sing	Fine Arts	Others	Total
Pre-WTO Period (1986-87 to 1994-95) (%)	-4.85	-8.98	-21.6	-2.80	2.53	-4.16	9.05	14.59	3.19	-15.9	0	9.70	-0.82	-1.94
Post-WTO Period (1995-96 to 1998-99) (%)	18.03	33.61	-17.8	76.63	34.76	25.87	-26.3	20.41	42.10	11.87	0.00	5.66	5.89	25.76
During Entire Period (1986-87 to 1998-99) (%)	-0.16	2.07	-8.22	9.74	13.20	7.04	-2.37	15.90	13.79	31.14	-8.30	5.94	2.71	5.87

Source: Table 6.8.

Fig. 6.6: Compound Growth Rates of Subject-wise Share of Indian Students Studying Abroad - Comparative Picture of Pre- and Post-WTO Period

and geographical conditions, nearer to native places and fees, living expenses are much cheaper than Western countries, have created conducive atmosphere for Asian students.

On the contrary to this, in recent years students from Asia are decreasing, because they are attracted towards Western nations; since Europe, America and Australia are aggressively marketing their education in global market. But students from American continent is increasing slowly, because students are interested in studying Indian culture, art, Architect, history, music, yoga etc., and above all, India has its own recognition in the world for its excellence in some specialized disciplines.

A comparative picture of students' inflow illustrates that, during pre-WTO period, American continent registered highest growth rate, followed by Africa and Asia, but Europe recorded negative growth rate and Oceania (Australia) continent registered zero growth. In case of post-WTO period American continent retained its first position but the percentage of growth was less than pre-WTO period; a significant growth rate registered for Asia and Australian continent; on the contrary negative growth rate is registered by Africa and European continent. It indicates that percentage of growth rate of students' mobility from Asia and Australian continents are increased towards India for higher studies during post-WTO period; on the other hand, percentage of growth rate of students' mobility from African continent decreased as compared to pre-WTO period; hence a negative growth rate is registered for the said period (*see* Fig. 6.7). As far as entire period is concerned, America recorded highest growth followed by Asia and Australia; on the other hand, Africa and European continents recorded negative growth.

Country-wise Inflow of International Students

The data presented in Table 6.10 explains the annual inflow of international students from selected countries of the world; the data reveals that majority of the foreign students are coming from developing countries particularly from Asian countries. Since India belongs to Asian continent factors like geographical region, historical connections to particular countries, economics of study and living have influenced students to choose India widely as preferred destination for their higher studies.

Table 6.9: Continent-wise Annual Inflow of International Students to India, 1986-87 to 2004-05

(in Numbers)

Year	*America*	*Europe*	*Asia*	*Oceania (Australia)*	*Others*	*Total*
1986-87	145	176	5390	49	5060	10820
	(1.34)	(1.63)	(49.82)	(0.45)	(46.77)	(100.00)
1987-88	158	165	5287	42	4921	10573
	(1.49)	(1.56)	(50.00)	(0.40)	(46.54)	(100.00)
1988-89	192	215	5605	48	5817	11877
	(1.62)	(1.81)	(47.19)	(0.40)	(48.98)	(100.00)
1989-90	193	195	6246	37	5833	12504
	(1.54)	(1.56)	(49.95)	(0.30)	(46.65)	(100.00)
1990-91	260	177	6124	35	6328	12924
	(2.01)	(1.37)	(47.38)	(0.27)	(48.96)	(100.00)
1992-93	153	155	5425	28	7030	12791
	(1.20)	(1.21)	(42.41)	(0.22)	(54.96)	(100.00)
1993-94	259	189	6125	36	7114	13723
	(1.89)	(1.38)	(44.63)	(0.26)	(51.84)	(100.00)
1994-95	431	124	5442	49	5850	11896
	(3.62)	(1.04)	(45.75)	(0.41)	(49.18)	(100.00)
1995-96	309	127	5530	40	4081	10087
	(3.06)	(1.26)	(54.82)	(0.40)	(40.46)	(100.00)
1996-97	163	91	2919	28	2680	5881
	(2.77)	(1.55)	(49.63)	(0.48)	(45.57)	(100.00)
1997-98	140	151	3839	35	2536	6701
	(2.09)	(2.25)	(57.29)	(0.52)	(37.85)	(100.00)
1998-99	124	111	2971	32	2085	5323
	(2.33)	(2.09)	(55.81)	(0.60)	(39.17)	(100.00)
1999-2000*	275	120	3804	31	2758	6988
	(3.94)	(1.72)	(54.44)	(0.44)	(39.47)	(100.00)
2000-01*	332	180	4063	44	3172	7791
	(4.26)	(2.31)	(52.15)	(0.56)	(40.71)	(100.00)
2001-02**	432	251	5054	45	2363	8145
	(5.30)	(3.08)	(62.05)	(0.55)	(29.01)	(100.0)
2002-03**	353	145	4451	40	2766	7755
	(4.55)	(1.87)	(57.40)	(0.52)	(35.67)	(100.00)
2003-04**	475	129	4822	42	2362	7830
	(6.07)	(1.65)	(61.58)	(0.54)	(30.17)	(100.00)

(Contd.)

Table 6.9: (*Contd.*)

Year	America	Europe	Asia	Oceania (Australia)	Others	Total
2004-05**	601 (4.57)	126 (0.96)	9779 (74.36)	55 (0.42)	2590 (19.69)	13151 (100.00)
Pre-WTO Period, CGR for 1986-87 to 1994-95 (%)	14.59	-4.28	0.12	0.00	1.83	1.19
Post-WTO Period, CGR for 1995-96 to 2004-05 (%)	6.88	-0.08	5.87	3.24	-4.45	2.69
Entire Period, CGR for 1986-87 to 2004-05 (%)	7.77	-1.74	3.18	0.61	-3.46	1.03

Source: 1. Indian Students/Trainees Going Abroad (various issues).
2. * Government of India, Selected Educational Statistics 2003-04, Ministry of Human Resource Development, p.113.
3. ** Compiled from the statistics released by: Lok Sabha Unstarred Question No. 40, dated 1-3-2005 and Lok Sabha Unstarred Question No. 4130, dated 22-4-2008.

Note: (1) 1991-92 data not available. (2) Figures in parenthesis indicate the percentage share for different continents.

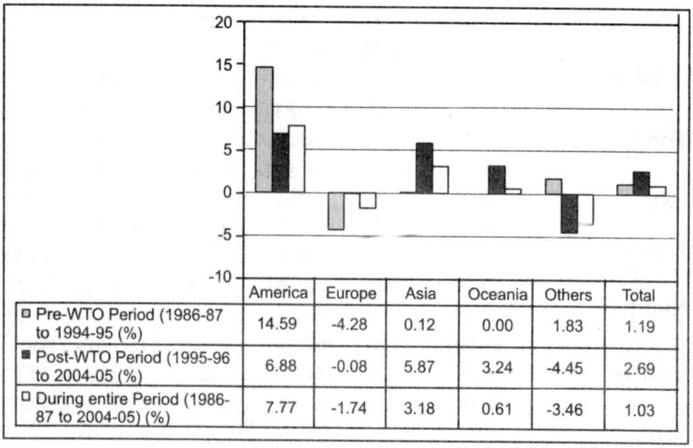

Source: Table 6.9.

Fig. 6.7: Compound Growth Rates of Annual Inflow of Students from Different Continents - A Comparative Picture of Pre- and Post-WTO Periods

The total number of students from the low income countries studying in India accounts major share in total overseas students in both pre- and post-WTO periods followed by middle income countries and high income countries. However, the total number of overseas students from low income countries declined during post-WTO period as compared to pre-WTO period. On the contrary to this, the growth of overseas students coming from low income countries is better in pre-WTO period as compared to post-WTO period; whereas the growth rate of overseas students from high income countries stood at first position followed by middle income countries.

During pre-WTO period, the low income countries viz. Afghanistan, Bangladesh, Nepal, Somalia and Sudan registered negative growth of overseas students from respective countries, but the condition was much worst during post-WTO period, because other countries viz. Indonesia, Ethiopia, Kenya and Uganda are added to negative growth category. It clearly indicates that students enrolled in India from low income countries are declining in recent years and they have diverted towards other countries. High income countries are sending more students to India for higher studies in recent years. During Pre-WTO period except Britain, France and Germany other high income countries registered positive growth, but during post-WTO period all countries have registered positive growth except Australia, France and Britain registered zero growth rate. As far as Middle Income countries are concerned, students from Fiji, Sri Lanka, South Korea, Jordan and Iran registered negative growth during pre-WTO period; except Jordan and Malaysia students from other countries have increased during post-WTO period (*see* Fig. 6.8).

The important observation is that, overseas students belonging to developed countries viz., USA, Germany, Canada, UAE, Japan and China are increasing in recent years. Bhalla Veena (2003) quoted that the increase in the number of students from the United States reflects the growing significance of Study Abroad Programmes in that country.

Students from low income countries are declining in recent years; the main reason for that is students are attracted towards western countries particularly USA, Germany, France, Britain, Canada and Australia, Switzerland etc. since these countries have adopted aggressive marketing strategies to trade their education services.

Countries belonging to Asian continent are sending more students; in this connection study of Mathang Seshagiri (2006) found that in

2004-05, the UAE sent 1500 students, followed by Nepal 1352 and Iran 1120; which shows that students from low and middle income countries are more keen studying in India because they find India as cost effective for higher studies, on the other hand, countries of African continent are in second position, but in recent years there is a sharp fall in the students from the African countries, viz., Kenya and Sudan.

International Students in Selected Universities of India

The data presented in Table 6.11 shows the annual inflow of overseas students to selected Indian universities; the University of Pune, the Manipal Academy of Higher Education and the University of Delhi are frontrunner in attracting more number of overseas students among other universities of the nation. These universities have good academic reputation and are more sensitive to the problems faced by overseas students in respective universities made them to attract more overseas students.

Indira Gandhi National Open University (IGNOU) has been steadily improving its position in attracting overseas students; during 2001-02 small number of overseas students was enrolled in IGNOU; later on in the year 2004-05 significant boost was observed in overseas students' enrollment. It indicates that IGNOU has good recognition and reputation in international level, which helps the IGNOU to market its educational programmes aggressively at international market.

Forecast of Growth in Overseas Students

The data presented in Table 6.12 are the outcome of the forecast study conducted by the British Council in UK on 'Vision 2020: Forecasting International Student Mobility'. The data reveals that, China is projected to be the biggest students in 2020, followed by Greece and Indian students respectively. Asia will be the fastest growing overseas students market, since China, Pakistan, India, Malaysia and Hong Kong will be the key growth drivers of the global demand for international higher education by 2020 A.D. Similarly, students of Western countries viz. Ireland, Greece, USA, Germany and France would also grow; further these countries would provide large market for higher education service providers; however the

Table 6.10: Country-wise Annual Inflow of International Students in India, 1986-87 to 2004-05

(in Numbers)

Country	1986-87	1987-88	1988-89	1989-90	1990-91	1992-93	1993-94	1994-95	1995-96	1996-97	1997-98	1998-99	1999-2000*	2000-01*	2001-02*	2002-03**	2003-04**	2004-05**	Pre-WTO Period, CGR for 1986-87 to 1994-95 (%)	Post-WTO Period, CGR for 1995-96 to 2004-05 (%)	Entier Period, CGR for 1986-87 to 2004-05 (%)
HIGH INCOME ECONOMIES																					
USA	98	110	127	137	198	106	201	362	251	129	102	87	223	246	331	244	354	398	17.74	4.72	7.66
Britain	63	75	111	70	70	49	62	45	47	27	33	26	40	51	96	54	55	47	-4.12	0.00	-1.53
France	37	24	22	30	22	36	35	10	12	8	13	14	18	23	49	15	12	11	-15.09	-0.87	-6.18
Germany	11	15	13	20	18	11	18	8	8	10	10	8	7	19	19	12	10	20	-3.90	9.60	3.20
Australia	6	6	10	8	15	6	10	17	12	7	7	8	9	17	21	11	17	9	13.90	-2.84	2.16
Canada	26	25	30	23	36	28	46	56	48	32	30	30	47	71	80	81	99	163	10.07	13.00	10.14
UAE	23	29	26	97	40	49	39	47	25	27	23	26	94	68	58	68	233	1500	9.34	50.60	24.59
Japan	38	18	19	35	23	27	34	52	46	45	50	38	43	48	65	51	45	63	4.00	3.19	2.70
China #	12	8	8	3	12	6	14	28	27	21	23	28	18	20	16	19	31	43	11.17	4.76	6.95
MIDDLE INCOME ECONOMIES																					
Mauritius	195	197	224	164	209	219	296	331	442	421	459	398	309	546	550	366	370	527	6.84	1.77	7.16
Fiji	40	33	32	24	17	22	24	31	25	19	27	21	3	21	13	4	19	37	-3.14	4.00	-7.22
Sri Lanka	586	705	430	552	540	487	420	369	363	348	420	368	485	383	504	391	355	582	-5.62	4.83	-1.00
Thailand	251	171	187	158	186	160	152	266	197	185	249	197	179	259	307	293	244	293	0.73	4.05	1.35
South Korea	9	4	9	16	1	18	20	0	22	72	26	19	65	23	38	14	29	242	-100.00	27.10	10.08
Malaysia	532	439	824	870	993	597	1421	1130	857	75	56	37	168	148	92	788	806	7	9.87	-38.17	-11.04
Oman	2	9	1	6	8	7	9	15	30	48	144	74	111	216	216	94	183	646	28.64	35.93	36.63
Jordan	906	1043	1247	1599	1506	1299	860	700	291	98	251	80	111	58	92	40	51	76	-3.17	-12.56	-14.14
Iran	742	628	553	404	370	348	338	393	240	201	163	108	151	217	245	336	472	1120	-7.64	16.65	-7.12

(Contd.)

Table 6.10: *(Contd.)*

Country	1986-87	1987-88	1988-89	1989-90	1990-91	1992-93	1993-94	1994-95	1995-96	1996-97	1997-98	1998-99	1999-2000*	2000-01*	2001-02*	2002-03**	2003-04**	2004-05**	Pre-WTO Period, CGR for 1986-87 to 1994-95 (%)	Post-WTO Period, CGR for 1995-96 to 2004-05 (%)	Entier Period, CGR for 1986-87 to 2004-05 (%)
LOW INCOME ECONOMIES																					
Afghanistan	162	146	153	140	113	125	111	100	71	105	84	59	46	35	33	24	25	35	-5.85	-6.83	-7.75
Bangladesh	266	244	252	362	399	565	736	129	1244	551	804	461	520	576	545	372	320	940	-8.65	-2.76	6.87
Indonesia	53	90	106	81	18	17	64	58	33	35	63	106	68	96	62	58	54	6	1.13	-15.67	-10.83
Korea	10	14	11	24	63	52	34	79	42	0	76	44	0	90	94	108	84	NA	29.48	8.01	12.55
Nepal	989	803	912	807	651	725	909	863	695	463	563	574	772	821	873	801	690	1352	-1.69	6.88	1.66
Ethiopia	193	296	455	476	488	674	685	632	302	204	301	403	369	301	281	225	351	226	15.98	-2.86	0.83
Kenya	1972	1902	2332	2856	3495	3980	4268	2951	2213	1246	992	639	868	968	548	521	454	418	5.17	-15.35	-7.84
Somalia	446	263	429	158	163	148	132	94	40	56	48	32	88	95	143	146	54	62	-17.69	4.48	-9.86
Sudan	1096	1400	1692	1633	1521	1657	1294	1004	450	378	350	245	299	381	301	186	188	150	-1.09	-10.40	-9.94
Uganda	54	46	31	48	60	57	98	297	275	183	208	196	199	240	132	93	53	70	23.75	-12.79	1.38

Source: 1. Indian Students/Trainees Going Abroad (various issues).
2. * Government of India, Selected Educational Statistics 2003-04, Ministry of Human Resource Development, p.113.
3. ** Compiled from the statistics released by: Lok Sabha Unstarred Question No.40, dated 1-3-2005 and Question No.4130, dated 22-4-2008.

Note: 1. # China, including Hong Kong; Symbol: ∞ includes both South Korea and North Korea.
2. Data on 1991-92 was not available.
3. Classification of Countries have been made on the bases of World Bank Report 2000.

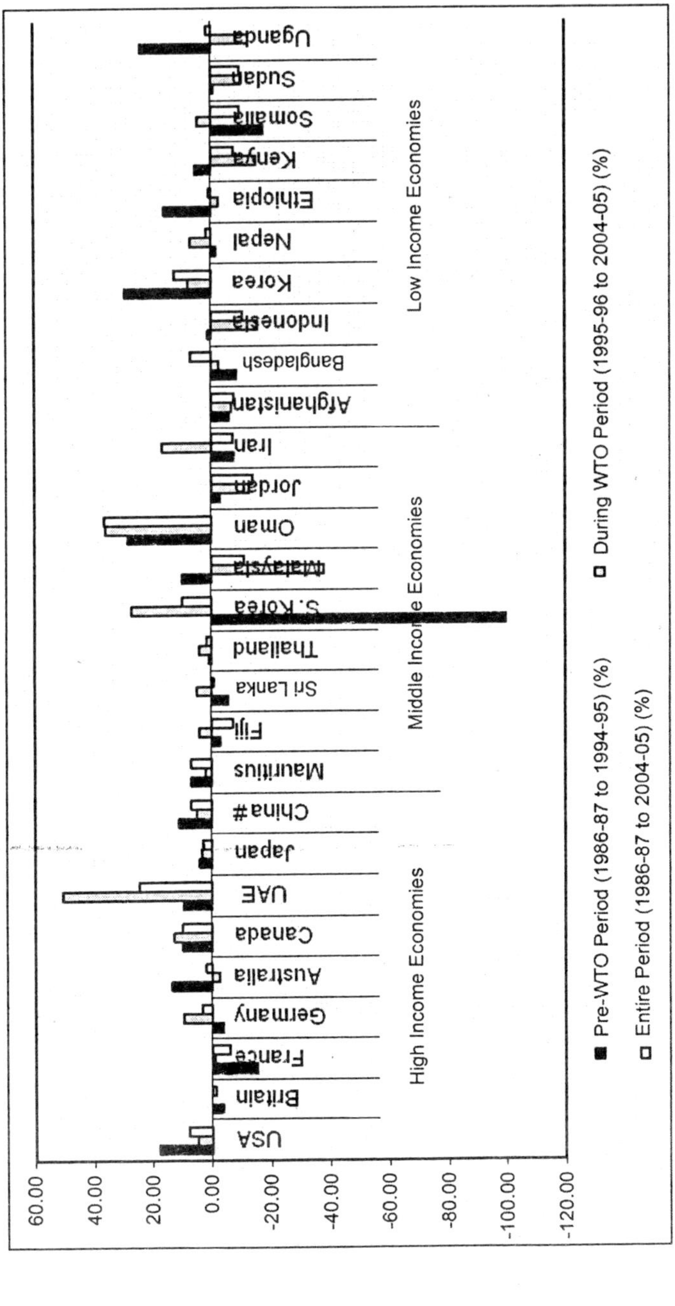

Source: Table 6.10.

Fig. 6.8: Compound Growth Rates of Annual Inflow of Students from Different Countries - A Comparative Picture of Pre- and Post-WTO Periods

Table 6.11: International Students in selected Top Universities of India, 1998-99 to 2004-05

(in Numbers)

No.	Universities	1998-99*	2001-02	2002-03	2003-04	2004-05
1.	University of Pune, Pune	402	1630	1048	1416	2144
2.	Manipal Academy of Higher Education (MAHE), Manipal	85	1070	1753	2031	1130**
3.	University of Delhi, Delhi	1405	1027	1083	1077	1003
4.	Osmania University, Hyderabad	103	380	435	186	279**
5.	University of Mysore, Mysore	NA	303	174	263	333
6.	Bharati Vidyapeeth, Pune	142	257	239	271	275**
7.	IGNOU, New Delhi	NA	205	120	452	963**
8.	University of Mumbai, Mumbai	186	182	152	121	77
9.	Banaras Hindu University, Varanasi	255	182	161	154	189
10.	Visva Bharati, Shantiniketan	NA	167	83	97	NA
11.	Jawaharlal Nehru University, New Delhi	NA	166	154	70	206
12.	Punjab University, Chandigarh	88	146	126	110	83
13.	Aligarh Muslim University, Aligarh	117	145	199	174	189
14.	Tilak Maharashtra Vidyapeeth, Pune	135	116	82	82	55
15.	Visveswaraiah Technological University, Belgaum	NA	107	151	99	NA
16.	Bharathiar University, Coimbatore	NA	102	65	42	NA
17.	University of Madras, Chennai	128	102	167	50	363**

Source: 1. * Indian Students/Trainees Going Abroad and Foreign Students in India (1998-99) .
2. Dr. Veena Bhalla, AIU.
3. **Seshagiri Mathang, *The Times of India*, December 7th, 2006.

Note: NA - Not Available.

percentage growth of overseas students are less compared to above-mentioned Asian countries.

A similar observation has been made by IDP Education Australia, 'The Global Student Mobility 2025' (2002), it estimates that at present there are 2 million students studying outside their home country; which is expected to grow more than three times, i.e. 7.2 million by 2025, with Asia dominating total Global demand at 70 per cent. Hence, India needs to implement the strategies for exploiting the opportunities by 2020.

Table 6.12: Forecast Growth in Overseas Students

Country	*2005*	*2010*	*2020*	*Compound Growth Rate from 2005 to 2020 (%)*
China	26,800	49,100	1,30,900	11.15
Greece	28,000	30,900	34,800	1.46
India	8,600	16,500	29,800	8.64
Malaysia	10,100	14,500	28,400	7.14
Ireland	12,800	14,800	17,900	2.26
USA	13,100	14,300	16,000	1.34
Germany	13,100	14,400	15,800	1.26
France	12,400	13,000	14,700	1.14
Hong Kong	9,100	10,800	14,000	2.91
Pakistan	2,800	4,800	11,100	9.62

Source: British Council Study.

The implications of consumption abroad mode to higher education is concerned, developed countries take full commitment; because it is obvious that their education institutions have competitive advantages with world class infrastructure facilities like library, hostels and well equipped laboratories and market oriented courses, international curricula etc. which have made them to attract more foreign students and earn huge amount of money. In case of India things are not up to the mark, however taking full commitment may have immense potentials for India to attract foreign students. Moreover, it provides multi-dimensional benefits such as improvement in the quality of education and infrastructure facilities, reducing students' outflow and earning huge foreign exchange in due course of time.

Reasons for the Phenomenal Growth in Student Mobility and Demand for Overseas Education

It is noticeable from the present research as well as other studies that the general patterns of global student mobility are influenced by the following wide variety of factors; these are going to answer the question why a particular international student might choose one destination country over another for study?

Natural factors: The geographical region of the world, historical connections of countries, language, culture, food patterns, education systems etc.

External factors: Implementation of LPG strategies, faster and better means of transport and communication facilities, inclusion of education in WTO's GATS agreements, increase in the per capita income and standard of living of the people, security to life and asset, maintenance of law and order, prestige and rewards attached to foreign degrees especially in developing countries, limited number of world class institutions; as Altbach Philip (2004) also made an similar observation that "Many of the world's brightest students seek opportunities abroad because there are few, if any, 'world-class' institutions in much of the world, especially in developing countries".

Academic factors: Acquisition of specialist knowledge and expose to world market, good infrastructure facilities at education institutions, desire to learn foreign language, cultures and to interact with foreigners, the perceived quality and reputation of the country's education provision,

Employment factors: Expectation of better career prospects, availability of market oriented courses, accessibility, affordability and the employability of the qualification obtained, to get a set of experiences that helps them to cope-up a diverse world, a diverse workplace.

C. Commercial Presence

Commercial Presence of service supply involves actual presence of Foreign Service provider in another (host) country, here education programmes and higher education institutions cross the border of a country, and mobility is motivated by the profit/income aspect. Population, demand for higher education in developing countries is increasing; which created huge market for higher education services; at the same time, most of the developed countries educational institutions are showing keen interest to establish their institutions in developing countries; through various means to utilize the available opportunities; where the developed countries have comparative advantage over developing courtiers in establishing/operating universities/institutions under commercial presence mode. It is observed that, already overseas higher education institutions are functioning in many developing countries and India is also not an exception for that.

Under Commercial Presence foreign/domestic education providers can show their presence in education market through four means viz. Franchisee[2], Programmatic Collaboration, Twinning Programmes and establishment of Branch/Independent Campus and *vice versa*. These forms of commercial presence may produce potential benefits to Indian higher education sector to certain extent e.g. it brings new courses, getting overseas degrees at cheaper rates, promote competitiveness among domestic providers etc. Similar observation has been made by Shollapur (2010) that the competition between the domestic and international universities/institutes would improve their quality, efficiency and accountability. On the other hand, it brings huge challenges/threats like participation of private/corporate may increase, neglect of basic traditional courses, duality of education (quality and access), internal brain drain of skilled educational service persons, adverse effects on public higher education, scope for departure of government support to education sector etc.

The number of Off-shore campuses is increasing in the world; the study by Becker (2009) shows that in 2009 there were as many as 189 international branch campuses; a 43 per cent increase in its number since 2008. The United States is followed by Australia, the United Kingdom and France are the main source countries; on the other hand, host countries include United Arab Emirates followed by Dubai, China, Singapore, Qatar and Malaysia; many of Arab countries are supported financially to Off-shore campuses. Fifty per cent of the branch campuses are from developed countries to developing countries (North to South). North to North provision is about 25 per cent; there has been a substantial increase in South to South provision (Becker, 2010; Pawar K. Sanjay, 2010). It indicates that developing countries are slowly but increasingly establishing their own branch campuses abroad. The large increase in South to South provision is largely due to the improved quality of higher education programmes in developing countries coupled with their increased ambition to export programmes and hopes to generate a profit from these ventures (Becker, 2010).

The data presented in Table 6.13 shows that South to South provision of branch campuses viz. sixteen Indian higher education institutions are functioning in various regions. Around 81 per cent of Off-shore campuses are functioning in Gulf region and almost all campuses are imparting Bachelors and Masters courses in professional areas; the programmes in business and management are mostly at the Master's level. The programmes in engineering and technology are at the Bachelor's level with a few vocational courses at certificate and diploma levels.

Off-shore campuses provide various benefits to foreign provider, the host country and to students; the following benefits are observed by Becker (2010). The foreign provider (1) generate substantial revenue through tuition fees and sale of learning materials; (2) gain international visibility as a provider of quality education; (3) provide their faculty with international teaching experience; (4) develop new and varied curriculum material; (5) increase its understanding of different cultures. The host country can benefit: (i) building of local capacities and educational infrastructure; (ii) reduction in outflow of foreign exchange and of brain-drain; (iii) internationalization of curricula and income generation for local business. Students also benefit: (a) having an opportunity to secure foreign degrees while staying at home; (b) get substantial savings because of lower tuition fees and saving on living expenses.

On the contrary, number of Off-shore campuses is closing in the world. There have been about a dozen case of closure because of lack of adequate number of students, and consequently financial non-viability. Closures have also been due to changed social-political situations (Pawar K. Sanjay, 2010). As a result of this source country instead of taking risks on Off-shore campuses; it is preparing for Programmatic Collaboration and Twinning Programme[4] with higher education institutions and government of host countries. As the FDI arrive into Indian education sector through commercial presence; where it has various implications to education sector; hence, Government of India should regulate the flow of FDI and using of 'National Regulations' to safeguard the public higher education; announcing/determination of the priority areas for foreign universities/ institutions are need of the hour.

Foreign Educational Institutional (Regulation of Entry and Operation) Bill, 2010

This bill (Bill No. 57 of 2010) was enacted in the Parliament of India; which provides various safeguard measures to higher education system. The bill requires foreign institution has to publish prospectus including of details of fees and deposits, number of seats available, admission process; further the disclosure of all matters regarding details of teaching faculty, their educational qualifications and

Table 6.13: Indian Universities and other HEIs having Off-shore Campuses[3]

Sl. No.	*University/HEI*	*Host Country and City*	*Year Opened*	*Level*	*Discipline*
1.	Manipal University, Manipal	Nepal, Pokhra	1994	Bachelors	Medicine (Articulation arrangement)
2.	Manipal University, Manipal	Malaysia, Melaka	1994	Bachelors	Medicine (Articulation arrangement)
3.	Birla Institute of Technology and Science, Pilani	UAE, Dubai IAC	2000	Bachelors	Engineering, Computer Science, Biotechnology
4.	Mahatma Gandhi University, Kottayam	UAE, Dubai IAC	2001	Bachelors Masters	Business, IT, Tourism, Fashion Technology
5.	Birla Institute of Technology, Mesra	Oman, Muscat	2003	Bachelors	Engineering
6.	Manipal University, Manipal	UAE, Dubai IAC	2003	Certificate Bachelors Masters	Engineering, Technology, Business, Design
7.	S.P. Jain Centre for Management, Mumbai	UAE, Dubai	2005	Masters	Business, Management
8.	S.P. Jain Centre for Management, Mumbai	Singapore	2006	Masters	Business, Management
9.	JSS Education Foundation, Bangalore	UAE, Dubai IAC	2006	Diploma, Certificate Masters	Engineering, Technology, Health Care Management
10.	Institute for Management Technology, Ghaziabad	UAE, Dubai IAC	2006	Masters	Business
11.	Welingkar Institute of Management Development and Research, Mumbai	UAE, Dubai IAC	2006	Post-graduate Diploma, Masters	Management
12.	Training and Advanced Studies in Management and Communication (IASMAC), Pune	UK, London	2008	Masters	Management
13.	Symbiosis International University, Pune	UAE, Dubai IAC	2009	Bachelors Masters	Business Administration, Management

(Contd.)

Table 6.13: (*Contd.*)

Sl. No	*University/HEI*	*Host Country and City*	*Year Opened*	*Level*	*Discipline*
14.	Bharati Vidyapeeth University, Pune	UAE, Ras Al Khaimah	2009	Bachelors Masters	Business
15.	University of Pune, Pune	UAE, Ras Al Khaimah	2009	Bachelors Masters	Business, Management
16.	Madurai Kamraj University, Madurai	UAE, Ras Al Khaimah	2009	Bachelors Masters	Business, Management, Technology

Source: Based on Becker, 2009.

teaching experience and pay categories, details of the institute of Physical and academic infrastructure, broad outlines of the syllabus and teaching hours. The 'foreign education institution' would be termed as 'foreign education provider' only after getting permission from the government; the foreign provider will have to make deposit of Rs. 50 crores as a corpus fund before setting up campuses. It has to offer academic programmes in conformity with those standards prescribed by the regulator and should be comparable to their offerings in their campuses in the country of their origin; it cannot send home surplus revenues; 75 per cent of revenues generated should be used for development of the institution in India and 25 per cent need to be deposited into the corpus fund. The bill provides for an eight-months time bound format for granting approval to a foreign institute to set up a centre in India through three levels—first the application is filed with the Registrar who approves it then approval is required from the higher education commission that will advise the centre, and finally the centre will take a call to grant or withhold the approval.

Possible Accomplishments

The following positive accomplishments are drawn from the bill: (1) a large amount of foreign direct investment (FDI) may enter into India; (2) high standard universities will come to India and provide access to high quality education to students, as students save the money; India will save foreign exchange. It is estimated that about 1,00,000 going abroad for studies, which is estimated to be around $75 billion a year (Tilak, 2010); (3) the entry of foreign institutions will lead to competition which improves the quality of education; (4) foreign education institutions are going to solve our problems viz. inadequate access, quality and funding in higher education.

The following negative accomplishments are drawn: (1) high standard foreign universities have not interest to come to India; they are much eager to take students to their home universities; (2) high standard universities are interested in collaboration with Indian universities as a part of Twinning and Programmatic Collaboration arrangements. Similar observation is made by Tilak (2010) that top ranking universities are interested in India, but only for collaboration in high quality research activities, and not for normal degree programmes; (3) the entry of foreign universities will result into unequal competition between foreign universities and domestic universities which produce unhealthy results; (4) foreign universities may not address our problems of higher education; (5) saving of huge foreign exchange may not be true.

D. Presence of Natural Persons

An annex of the GATS deals with the movement of natural persons and with negotiations on the right of individuals to stay temporarily in a country for the purpose of providing a service. It does not facilitate to obtain permanent employment or citizenship and permanent residence. This mode of supply occurs when a service is provided by someone who has moved into the territory of the consumer. It includes both the self-employed who supply direct services and employees who go abroad temporarily in connection with the supply of a service while still employed by an enterprise in their home country.

It is difficult to estimate the impact of temporary labour migration on home and host countries. The impact is specific to the type of labour in question, the sector receiving or sending the labour, the regulations in place, and many other factors that may vary across countries. It also depends on whether movement of labour is the sole means of delivering the services, whether it complements or facilitates trade in other modes such as commercial presence, and whether it can be replaced by other modes of supply. There are both costs and benefits to the countries sending and receiving the labour.

The temporary mobility of Teachers, Professors, Researchers, Technical faculty and Non-technical faculties abroad is observed in education sector. Since many Teachers, Professors and Researchers want to move to countries with more favourable working conditions and salaries, there is real concern that most developed countries will benefit from this type of mobility.

The Indian perspective, foreign educational workers (Teachers, Professors and Researchers etc.,) inflow may promote specialization and economics of scale and scope, also the transfer of skills and knowledge embodied in foreign educational workers are expected gains. On the contrary, it may reduce the ōpportunities for domestic qualified eligible talents.

As far as the outflow of Indian educational workers is concerned, it may reduce pressure on domestic employment market and solve problem of unemployment among the educated youths; since a large pool of eligible teaching talent already available in our country. Sharma Sheetal (2006) observed that, every year approximately 17,000 candidates become eligible for teaching positions at college or universities, through UGC-JRF/NET/CSIR JRF-NET/SLET along with those who are exempted from NET, but compete for only few thousand positions. Hence, the surplus eligible teaching candidates can utilize an opportunity to serve abroad under this mode. Besides there will be offsetting gains in the form of experience, skills gained abroad and remittances. But at the same time, there may be temporary loss of specialized domestic skills and experts, however, comparing with permanent labour outflow (brain-drain) this temporary outflow costs likely to be smaller.

Further, the gains need to be weighed against costs due to displacement of domestic workers, costs in the form of social security, health care, and education. However, such costs are generally smaller in the case of temporary foreign workers. The balance of costs and benefits also depend on the regulatory framework of the recipient country. The extent to which costs can be lowered or skills can be transferred depends on the conditions that are enforced on foreign workers. Foreign suppliers may be forced to comply with domestic arrangements on wages, prices, and taxes which could erode their economic advantage and reduce the scope for trade. They may also be denied access to certain specified activities or forced to fulfil additional requirements, thus limiting the scope for transfer of skills and knowledge. Hence, the regulatory environment is critical to determining the scope and implications of trade in services through the temporary movement of labour.

Restrictions/Barriers

There are numerous restrictions/barriers which can be imposed for determining the temporary mobility of labour; but it is difficult to quantify and even identify barriers to the temporary migration of labour. They relate mainly to domestic regulations and are therefore mostly administrative in nature. The following are the few important regulations/barriers for presence of natural persons.

Immigration Related Regulations

The immigration and labour market policies of individual countries will determine the entry and stay of natural persons. The variety of restrictions may be employed for controlling the mobility of natural persons, such as stringent eligibility conditions for applications of work permits/visas, cumbersome procedures for actual application and processing of these visas/permits, limitations on the duration of stay and transferability of employment in the overseas market. As far as duration of stay (visas) for service providers is valid only for specific period and it can be often extendable, renewable subject to tough conditions and high fees.

Apart from immigration-related restrictions on entry and stay, there is also host of entry barriers in the form of additional requirements imposed on Foreign Service Providers. These include economic needs tests, local market tests, and management needs test to ascertain the need for entry as well as the number to be allowed to enter.

Regulations Concerning Recognition, Certification, and Licensing

Movement of natural persons in services is also constrained by requirements on qualifications, work experience, and licensing/certification. Recognition requirements may either prevent market access for the foreign service provider causing a rejection of work permit or visa application, or may limit his scope for work to specific activities once he enters the overseas market. The nationality requirement is used as barrier on the basis of citizenship, residency based requirements of service professionals. Further, nationality requirement is used as key criteria for granting recognition to natural persons and for determining the scale of their activities in certain service sectors. Sometimes, in the absence of formal certification, licensing procedures to accord recognition, work experience and educational qualifications would be used for granting recognition.

These regulations are treated as consumer protection and nation interest concerns; by laying code of conduct to particular professions these may prevent damage to consumers and nation interest and also maintain high quality service in many sectors.

Differential Treatment of Domestic and Foreign Service Personnel

As a matter of social security point of view foreign service personnel are treated differentially. In this connection Chanda Rupa (1999) observed that, there is differential treatment for temporary service providers in the context of social security taxes and benefits in United States (US). For instance, temporary service providers in the US economy are required to make social security payments like Mediclaim and FICA taxes to the US Government in the absence of tax treaties between the home country and the US.

Government Subsidies and Government Procurement are used for treating differently to domestic and foreign service persons. These are often used for protecting the domestic service providers of public goods. Chanda Rupa (1999) quoted that, Discriminatory government procurement regulations and price-based preferences granted to domestic suppliers are common in areas such as education, data processing, and non-medical professional services. In some cases, government subsidies and procurements are introduced for the sake of national interest and not for preventing the entry of foreign service personnel in specific sectors.

Thus, there are numerous regulations and policies which affect the movement of natural persons in services. Many of these regulations affect developing country's trade in service sectors where they have export potential. The direct or indirect effect of these regulations is to raise costs of entry and operation for service providers, reduce the scope for technology and skill transfer, and force substitution of domestic with foreign service personnel.

Opportunities and Challenges to India Under Four Modes of Trade in Higher Education Services

Table 6.14 illustrates the mode-wise analysis of trade in higher education services. The trading of educational services under four modes has both opportunities and challenges for India. As far as challenges are concerned, the essential strategies are suggested to translate the challenges in opportunities and capitalize on the opportunities. Further, table critically evaluates the mode-wise Opportunities and Challenges of trade in higher education services on India's point of view as Exporter and Importer. It observed that, under mode III i.e. 'Commercial Presence' India will face huge challenges/threats; therefore strict regulation mechanism should be taken and in case of 'Cross Border Supply' India will benefit if it utilizes its well developed ICT sector. As far as 'Consumption Abroad' and 'Presence of Natural Persons' modes are concerned India remains at competitive advantage position. Hence, in all these respects the required actions (promotions/regulations) are suggested for capitalizing the opportunities of WTO's GATS agreements.

Conclusion

From the foregoing analysis, it may be concluded that, as far as implications of Cross Border Supply mode is concerned; India has potential to grow internationally with its well developed ICT sector; by popularizing its Distance Education Programmes/Courses, India can get recognition internationally, particularly in developing countries.

Further, the facts related to student mobility, provided the status of foreign students' inflow and Indian students' outflow from mid-80s (1986-87) to twenty first century (2001-02). It is observed that, the number of students going abroad far exceed those coming to India. It is strongly felt that, India has to adopt various strategies to encourage the inflow of foreign students from different parts of the world. As far as implications of consumption abroad mode to higher education is concerned, developed countries take full commitment in mode II, because it is obvious that their education institutions have competitive advantages with world class infrastructure facilities like library, hostels and well equipped laboratories and market oriented courses, international curricula etc. have been able to attract foreign students

Table 6.14: Mode-wise Analysis of Opportunities and Challenges

Modes	*Opportunities*	*Challenges*	*Actions Needed Regulations / Promotions*
1. Cross Border Supply	• Prospects for tele-education in management & executive training		
Supply side (Exporter)	• Education process outsourcing with distant tutoring		
Demand side (Importer)	• Expands accessibility	• Monitor of programme content • Flood of unrecognized private education providers	• Seeking permission should be mandatory before entering the market • Course and course content should strictly examined and then permitted • Restriction on improper electronic (internet) transmission • Excessive fees/taxes imposed on licensing payments
2. Consumption Abroad			
Supply side (Exporter)	• Improvement in quality of domestic education institutions	• Development & maintenance of world-class infrastructure facilities	• Easing admission procedures • Easing visa procedures
Foreign students inflow	• Improvement in infrastructural facilities • Earning of foreign exchange	• Scarcity of market oriented courses	• Providing incentives, scholarships/fellowships • Allowing students to work while studying

(*Contd.*)

Table 6.14: *(Contd.)*

Modes	*Opportunities*	*Challenges*	*Actions Needed Regulations / Promotions*
	• Getting special knowledge and skills		• Regulation on mobility
Demand side (Importer) Indian students outflow			• Restrictions on release of bank loan, foreign exchange
3. Commercial Presence			
Supply side (Exporter)	• Institutions will get international level recognition • Setting up of overseas campuses Reputation will increase	• Lagging in advertisements	• Providing exclusive subsidies to domestic providers
	• Inflow of FDI in higher education sector	• Quality of public education may deteriorate	• Limitations on number of campuses
Demand side (Importer)	• Possible to maintain the balance between demand and supply	• Threat for quality, equity and accessibility	• Limitations on number of programmes
	• Reduces students' outflow • Competition will increase • Provides new technologies • Provides new curriculum	• Possibility of uneven growth of foreign providers • Possibility of commercialization of education	• Agency should be set up for reorganization of institutions • Limitations on FDI • Imposing high licensing fees

(Contd.)

Table 6.14:(*Contd.*)

Modes	*Opportunities*	*Challenges*	*Actions Needed Regulations / Promotions*
	• Students get foreign degrees	• Occurrence of dual market • Possibility of internal brain-drain	• Much liberalization is facilitated for only Priority areas • Quality check up mechanism must be set up & strengthened
4. Movement of Natural Persons Supply side (Exporter)	• Provides global exposer • Skill/Technical improvements • Reduces pressure on domestic job market • Earning of foreign exchange	• Occurrence of brain-drain • Loss of specialized experts	• Specialized experts should be retained through legislations
Demand side (Importer)	• Provides new teaching/learning process • Facilitate more interaction • Service of expertise foreign faculty	• Occurrence of domestic displacement	• Restrictions on recruitment of foreign teachers and researchers, etc. • Fixing quota on number of temporary staff • Nationality or Residence requirements • Economic need test • Making complexity in obtaining authorization to enter & leave the country • Imposing costly fees/taxes for currency conversion

and earn huge amount of money. But in case of India, things are not up to the mark. However, taking full commitment and developing institution to offer world class higher education service may have immense potentials to attract foreign students. Moreover, it provides multi-dimensional benefits such as improvement in the quality of education and infrastructure facilities thereby attract more foreign students, reducing students' outflow and earning huge foreign exchange in due course of time.

Under the Commercial Presence mode India will face huge challenges and in this case, very strict regulation mechanism should be implemented to protect the domestic higher education system. As fas as the implication of mode IV is concerned India has competitive advantage over others with large pool of skilled and semi-skilled human resource in general and in particular education service providers.

NOTES

1. These are the four modes of supply of education services; under the cross border supply the provision of a service where the service crosses the border; it excludes the physical movement of the consumer. Consumption Abroad means the provision of the service where the consumer to the country of the supplier; it means students mobile from one country to another for acquiring the higher education. Commercial Presence indicates the provision of a service where the provider establishers or has presence in, commercial facilities in another country in order to render service. Presence of Natural Persons means the provision of a service where a people travel to another country on a temporary basis to provide the service.
2. Franchisee is one where home country institutions grant the permission to host country institutions to execute their programme with their name, curriculum, and evaluation methods. Home country institution/ university ties up with host country partner which acts as 'Study and Examination Centre' to deliver their course and also conduct the examination for the same.
3. Off-shore Campuses/Branch/Independent Campus is purely commercial operation and FDI arrive into the host country education sector, where foreign institutions have maximum stake under branch campus, here the home (foreign) country/university may open its branch either as its sole subsidiary or in partnership with the host

country institution. In this mode programmes, institutions and faculty mobile to host country, but teachers (faculty) mobile partly.

4. Programmatic Collaboration is one of the cheapest ways to earn foreign degree; here teacher as well as student exchange occurs. It enables a student to complete study in host country institutions and get a joint degree i.e. (host as well as home country education institutions). A student can complete study in India and get a joint degree.

   Twining Programmes facilitate students to earn foreign degree at least cost with outside exposure; here students can complete part of their study in host and part in home country's university; and only students travel from host to home country, but institutions and programmes remain in their places.

7

Summary of Findings and Important Suggestions

Introduction

The WTOs GATS agreements are increasingly affecting the global trade in services and trade in education services are not exception for that. The Government of India has supreme authority over its international trade relations and commitment; it should first start and implement domestic reforms in education sector (universities/institutions) by redefining its structure, working, courses and curricula, management, finance and infrastructure. So that it strengthens its education system for meeting the challenges of GATS successfully; further it can utilize the opportunities for achieving quality, competence in education by increasing its accessibility. True impact of GATS agreements is only to be seen in the coming years as India recently enacted the Foreign Educational Institutions (Regulation of Entry and Operations) Bill.

The opening of higher education to WTO's GATS would bring thrilling changes and add a new dimension to the structure of higher education. In view of this an attempt has been made to overview the World Trade Organization (WTO), General Agreement on Trade in Services (GATS) and summary of the commitment made by WTO's member nations on education sector. An analysis relating to the GATS article-wise implications on Indian higher education is provided. Further, the mode-wise analysis viz. Cross Border Supply, Consumption Abroad, Commercial Presence and Presence of Natural Persons of trade in higher education services and the data on trends of Foreign Students 'Inflow and Indian Students' Outflow by year-wise, sex-wise, subject-wise, country-wise, continent-wise, source of financial assistance for outflow are analyzed in detail, further opportunities and challenges of higher education services are evaluated. The study is based on secondary data collected from the various reports on the different aspects of foreign students' inflow and Indian students' outflow by the Ministry of Human Resource Development (MHRD) of the Indian Students/Trainees Going Abroad, the Selected Educational Statistics and other documents. The simple statistical tools viz. compound annual growth rates (CGR) averages and percentages have been used. The important findings of the study are summarised as follows:

Growth and Present Status of Higher Education System

India has the rich inheritance, magnetic qualities and profundity of knowledge from the dawn of civilization. During ancient period number of intellectual learned scholars visited India to enrich and fulfil their thirst for knowledge; on the other hand, number of foreign students studied in our ancient universities viz. Nalanda, Vallabhi and Vikramshila are renowned as international centres of learning.

There has been a considerable increase in the spread of higher educational institutions in the country since 1950-51 to 2009-10; the growth of colleges is much faster than the universities; there is around 15 times increase in universities and about 45 times boost in colleges during the referred period. As observed during sixties and seventies the growth rate of both higher education institutions and student enrolment was higher; growth of enrolment was all times high during 1970-71; which is highest in entire decades (1950-51 to 2009-10), also it was much higher than education institutions. It is observed that both the institutions and enrolment are not growing at uniform rate. The growth of students is much faster than teachers in entire decades (1950-51 to 2009-10); but during 1990-91 growth rate of teachers was registered negative. The huge difference between the growth of students and teachers has led to poor Student-Teacher Ratio (STR) at higher education level.

State Universities contributing immensely to higher education in the country; it is predicted that in future the number of Deemed-to-be-Universities and State Private Universities are going to increase in the country. Very small number of women colleges are functioning in the country; i.e. around 1/10 portion of total number of colleges is imparting education. Majority of women have opted Arts and Humanities discipline for higher studies; followed by Science, Commerce/Management and Engineering/Technology and Medicine courses respectively. However, it is a matter of great concern that, women enrolment is very small for Management, Engineering/Technology, Medicine, even though these fields are in great demand. During all the referred periods (1961-62 to 2008-09) majority of doctoral degrees awarded belong to Arts and Science subjects. These two faculties together accounted for 66 per cent of the total number of doctoral degrees awarded in 2008-09. It is observed that quantum of plan allocation for higher education is depending on the decision regarding the quantum of plan allocation for elementary education.

GATS Implications on Indian Higher Education System

As far as implication of WTO's GATS agreements on higher education sector is concerned, the articles namely 'Market Access', 'National Treatment', 'Domestic Regulations' and 'Recognition' play an important role for determining the size of higher education market; and further, these articles facilitate to control the entry/functioning of fake and sub-standard foreign universities/institutions in domestic higher education market. The WTO and GATS agreements widen the higher education sector by reducing the barriers/restrictions on movement of students, teachers, capital and goods. There is a possibility of either reduction/drop/removal in government support for public higher education institutions or the Government of India should extend its support to foreign education institutions keeping in view the GATS agreements and their bindings.

The study observed that India has huge opportunities to grow and maximize the benefits in trade in higher education services under Mode I, Mode II and Mode IV; whereas under Mode III India will face huge challenges/threats. Under Mode I, i.e. 'Cross Border Supply' India has potential to grow. On the one hand, it brings more relevant age group of India under higher education by expanding its coverage through starting/establishing Distance Learning Centres, Virtual Universities, and Corresponding Courses etc. On the other hand, Foreign Distance Education Providers also expands higher education coverage; in this case, India should adopt strict monitoring mechanism for recognizing course, course content, quality of programmes etc. for disqualifying the sub-standard providers.

During pre- and post-WTO periods, fluctuating trends were observed in foreign students' inflow. However, during pre-WTO period foreign students' inflow was high and increasing as compared to post-WTO period. Hence, during pre-WTO period, the foreign students' inflow to India registered positive growth (1.19%); where in post-WTO period, the growth of foreign students' inflow to India was negative (–3.50%).

As far as, the outflow of Indian students is concerned; during pre-WTO period small number of students was going abroad for higher studies. But during post-WTO period, students going abroad have been continuously increasing; and a substantial increase is registered during 1999-2000 to 2001-02. It indicates that due to liberalization policies, aggressive marketing strategies of Western countries attracted more Indian students towards their universities/ institutions. During pre-WTO period Indian students' outflow registered negative growth (–1.94%); but during post-WTO period unprecedented growth was registered in Indian students' outflow (71.34%). As fas as sex-wise outflow of Indian students is concerned, male students have major share in total outgoing students in both pre and post-WTO period. However, the growth of male students outflow was negative during pre-WTO period; but in post-WTO period positive growth was registered. Even though, outgoing female students account a small portion as compared to outgoing male students; the growth rate of outgoing female students is higher than the male students in both pre- and post-WTO periods. During pre-WTO period, the small per cent of growth was registered in female students; which significantly increased in post-WTO period. It clearly depicts that female students are now enjoying more liberty and equal opportunities as compared to earlier days in accessing for higher education.

During both pre- and post-WTO periods, major portion of outgoing Indian students have chosen American continent for their higher studies; consequently, American continent stands at the top position in attracting Indian students; whereas the Australia and European continents are almost at second and third place in this respect. The three continents viz. America, Europe and Australia (Oceania) put together account highest percentage of the Indian students in pre- and post-WTO periods; leaving thereby, a very small fraction of students to Asia and African continents. During pre-WTO period, the Australian continent registered highest growth rate in attracting Indian students, followed by Europe and Asia; on the other hand, American continent registered negative growth rate (-6.77%). During post-WTO period almost all continents of the world are attracting more Indian students towards their universities; at the same period American continent registered significant growth in attracting Indian students followed by Asia, Europe and Australia. The Australia and European continents are emerging in international education market and they are providing stiff competition to America in attracting overseas students during post-WTO regime. The most of the Indian students have chosen high income countries as their favoured destination for their higher studies during both pre- and post-WTO periods. During pre- and post-WTO periods, countries belong to high income category registered higher growth rate in attracting Indian students. The middle income countries viz. Malaysia, Thailand, Philippines and Hungary are showing keen interest in attracting Indian students during post-WTO period.

As far as state-wise Indian students outflow is concerned, the middle income states of India are sending more students abroad; accounting more than 50 per cent in all years of both pre- and post-WTO periods. Particularly Tamil Nadu, Andhra Pradesh and Karnataka are sending more students. On the other hand, the states belonging to high income category stand in second position and low income states are at third position among the total outgoing Indian students.

It is found that, majority of Indian students went abroad through unidentified financial sources; followed by self-financed sources; which means that group of students went abroad for higher studies through their own expenses during both per- and post-WTO periods. Further, the remaining sources of finance (viz. Scholarships and free-ship offered by foreign institutions, Expenses met by Indian/foreign companies etc.) have not significantly influenced or contributed to students' outflow for pursuing their higher studies during said period. As far as distribution of Indian students by fields of studies is concerned, in both pre- and post-WTO period the three fields of studies viz. (i) Engineering and Architect, (ii) Science, Technology and Industry and (iii) Commerce, Business Administration/ Management have absorbed around 60 per cent to 70 per cent of Indian students. During pre-WTO period majority of Indian students went abroad for higher studies by choosing courses Engineering and Architect, and Science these stands first and second position respectively. The number of students choosing the course of

Technology and Industry increased significantly during post-WTO period; it registered 76.63 per cent growth rate, which is highest among other subjects.

As far as foreign students studying in Indian universities is concerned; the students belonging to Asia and African Continents are representing major portion of overseas students in India during both pre- and post-WTO periods. However, steep decline is observed in overseas students of African continent during post-WTO period; as they are attracted towards Western countries. The number of students coming from America and Asian continents studying in Indian universities/institutions is increasing during post-WTO period; because they are coming to study some unique courses like Yoga, Art and Architect, Ayurveda, Music, Indian Culture and History etc; where India has its own recognition in the world for its excellence in these specialized disciplines/areas. During post-WTO period, students of African continent to India registered negative growth rate; it indicates that students from African continents are coming in less number and they are diverted toward Western countries. The total number of students from the low income countries studying in India accounts major share in total overseas students in both pre- and post-WTO periods followed by middle income countries and high income countries. However, the total number of overseas students from low income countries are declining during post-WTO period compared to pre-WTO period. On the contrary to this, the growth of overseas students coming from low income countries are better in pre-WTO period as compared to post-WTO period; whereas the growth rate of overseas students from high income countries stood at first position followed by middle income countries. During pre-WTO period, the low income countries viz. Afghanistan, Bangladesh, Nepal, Somalia and Sudan registered negative growth of overseas students from respective countries, but the condition was much worst during post-WTO period, because other countries viz. Indonesia, Ethiopia, Kenya and Uganda are added to negative growth category. It clearly indicates students enrolled in India from low income countries are declining in recent years and they diverted towards other countries. High income countries are sending more students to India for higher studies in recent years. During pre-WTO period except Britain, France and Germany other high income countries registered positive growth, but during post-WTO period all countries have registered positive growth except Australia, France and Britain registered zero growth rate. As far as Middle Income countries are concerned, students from Fiji, Sri Lanka, South Korea, Jordan and Iran registered negative growth during pre-WTO period; except Jordan and Malaysia, students from other countries are increasing during post-WTO period.

As far as foreign students studying in selected top universities of the country is concerned, the well-known universities of India viz. University of Pune, Manipal Academy of Higher Education (MAHE) and University of Delhi are attracting good number of overseas students among other universities of the country. It is because of the fact that, these have good academic reputation and are more sensitive to problems faced by overseas students. The number of overseas students studying in IGNOU is steadily increasing (2001-02 to 2004-05); it clearly indicates that courses and programmes of IGNOU are getting more name and fame at international level. As far as forecasted growth of overseas students in the world is concerned; the highest growth of overseas students are aspiring to study abroad will be from Asian continent; particularly China, Pakistan, India and Malaysia by 2020. It depicts that Asian continent will be hub of students; who are interested to study abroad by 2020.

As far as Commercial Presence Mode is concerned, India is at receiving end; it faces huge challenges viz. entry of sub-standard Universities/Institutions, threat for domestic Universities/Institutions, commercialization of higher education, occurrence of dual market, threat for quality, equity and accessibility etc. India has competitive advantage under Mode IV i.e. 'Presence of Natural Persons'; India can utilize its huge Skilled and Semi-skilled manpower in general and educational workers in particular for earning huge foreign exchange by sending them abroad; it can ease the pressure on domestic employment market, provides job opportunities, international level exposure and improves the income and standard of living of service personnels.

Policy Suggestions

The quantitative expansion of higher education institutions have not sufficient condition for imparting higher education; it should be simultaneously followed by quality, accessibility and equity. Student enrolment in higher education institutions has substantially increased for last sixty years. However, the coverage of relevant age-group (18-23) under higher education is very little. The issue of inclusion of disadvantaged section of the society under higher education segment is required in order to provide the benefits of higher education. The STR is an important factor to determine the quality of education; the government should recruit more teachers and fill up the all vacant posts to attain ideal STR at higher education level. The Government has accepted higher education as a merit good and continues to fund it. However, the financial situation is worried and in need of a quick solution. Domestic Institutions/Universities need to increase their seat reservation limit for foreign students along with encouraging the self-financing students; which promote inflow of foreign students. Further introduction of international level infrastructure facilities viz. up-dated and internationalized curriculum, market oriented courses (short-term courses and certificate courses), well equipped laboratories, library, hostels etc. help to strengthen Domestic Institutions/Universities capacity.

The articles of GATS are much complicated having variety of implications for Indian higher education; hence thorough study on the issue is required to be conducted. In this connection, more research should be conducted to derive the possible implications of GATS on Indian higher education sector and asking for recommending the policy measures regarding the issue. Further, the conduct of Seminar, Conferences and Public Debate on the issue is required; and the information and data related to the trade in education services should be made available at public domine for reference. Basically, the general obligation of GATS apply to all its member nations; whereas specific commitments on higher education sector is concerned these apply only to those members who have committed particular (higher education) service sector under GATS and hence articles such as 'Market Access', 'Domestic regulations', and 'Recognition' play dominant role in determining the size and scope of the (higher education) market.

The study observed that, distance mode of education has great potential to grow in future and will succeed in covering huge relevant age-group (18-25) population under higher education. Hence, India has to utilize its potential area of ICT sector for expanding the higher education coverage within and outside the country and harnessing the benefits of opportunities available under GATS through Cross Border Supply mode. Liberalization policies under WTO have paved the way for increase in students' mobility; in this connection, India should redefine its higher education policy to accommodate the WTO agreements on the one hand; and it should implement aggressive advertising/marketing policies for attracting more foreign students on the other hand.

The world class Institutions/Universities should be established with full-fledged facilities. While it retains Indian students and saves valuable foreign exchange on the one hand; it attracts foreign students to India; which have spillover effects on Indian higher education system. It is found that, majority of students went abroad for studying Technical and Management courses and demand for graduates in these fields is increasing. Hence, at this juncture, Institutions/Universities related to these field of studies should be established with international level facilities; side by side the existing well-known Domestic Institutions/Universities viz. IITs, IIMs, IGNOU, Central Universities, known as State Universities etc. should improve their standards by implementing state-of-the-art technologies; so that to attract more foreign students and retain its domestic students going abroad. India should concentrate on developing countries, particularly on Asian and African continents for attracting their students without neglecting developed countries of the world; because it is forecasted that the growth of overseas students in Asia will be more than 35.51 per cent by 2020; which will be highest among other continents.

The Commercial Presence Mode has to be dealt with cautiously in order to prevent the entry of sub-standard institutions/universities and degradation of education; in this connection declaration/ recognition of priority fields for foreign education institution entry/ operation should be clearly announced on the consultation of experts, specialists of the respective fields and wide range of public discussions. The proper regulatory mechanism (body) should be set up for monitoring the activities and examining the proposed course and course content, so that only accredited and well-known foreign institutions enter into the Indian market. Further, it should be made mandatory for foreign institutions/universities for getting clearance from respective authorities; with minimum required infrastructure, qualified faculty, etc; further the fees and donations charged by them should also be controlled and regulated. Along with this, the High Commission/Embassies of India have to get information from concerned countries regarding the background and credibility of Foreign Educational Institutions; who are interested to function in India; which serve the purpose.

It is found that, India has comparative advantage in Mode IV, with huge potential skilled and semi-skilled manpower resources. Therefore, making full commitment in this mode will be beneficial for the country. In this regard, the Government of India and related agencies should discuss/negotiate the issue at national and international level with suitable measures and agreements; further providing of 'Temporary Migrant Visa' facility should be implemented by all member nations of the WTO for which our country has to take care and efforts.

It is a strong felt need that, maintenance of database on operation of Foreign Educational Institutions in the country (including Open/ Virtual Institutions), foreign students 'inflow and Indian students' outflow and temporary mobility of Indians/foreigners (service providers) in particular education migrants, which help to draw a suitable measures for maximizing the fruits of liberalization in education sector.

Bibliography

A. Besant C. Raj (2004). Higher Education as a Lever of Development, in Venkatasubramanian K. (ed.), *Issues in Higher Education, Vol.I*, Hyderabad: The ICFAI University Press.

Agarwal, P. (1999). External Brain Drain: An Opportunity for Trade in Services Sector for India. *University News*, 37 (28).

Agarwal, P. (2006). Higher Education Policy: Many Contradictions. *Economic and Political Weekly*, Vol.XLI (45): 4645-4648.

Agarwal, V. and U.R. Sharma (2004). Privatization Vs. Commercialisation of Higher Education: Some Facts, Concerns and Suggestions. *University News*, 42 (07).

Agrawal, R. (2004). Privatization in the Context of Globalization, WTO and GATS in Indian Scenario. *University News*, 42 (07).

Ahmad, Nighat (2004). Global Student Mobility: Opportunities and Challenges for India. *University News*, 42 (50).

Ahmad, Nighat (2005). WTO and Higher Education Challenges and Opportunities for India. *88th Annual Conference Volume, Indian Economic Association (IEA)*: 156-165.

Akhtar, S.W. (2012). Quality in Higher Education at Par with International Standards. *University News*, 49 (52): 01-02.

Altbach, G. Philip (1982). *Higher Education in the Third World: Themes and Variations.* Regional Institute of Higher Education and Development. Maruzen, Asia.

Altbach, G. Philip (1999). The Perils of Internationalizing Higher Education. *University News*, 37 (27): 01-02.

Altbach, G. Philip (2000). The Crisis in Multinational Higher Education. *University News*, 38 (45): 08-09.

Altbach, G. Philip (2003). Globalization and the University Myths and Realities in an Unequal World. *Journal of Educational Planning and Administration*, XVII (02).

Altbach, G. Philip (2010). *Why Branch Campuses may be Unsustainable*. International Higher Education, The Boston College Centre for International Higher Education, 58, Winter 2010: 02-03.

Altbach, G. Philip and Umakoshi Toru (Eds.), (2004). *Asian Universities: Historical Perspectives and Contemporary Challenges*. Johns Hopkins University Press, Baltimore and London.

Anandakrishnan, M. (2004). Internationalization of Higher Education: Policy Concerns. Paper presented at National Conference on *"Internationalization of Higher Education: Issues and Concerns"* held at National Institute of Educational Planning and Administration (NIEPA), New Delhi.

Azad, J.L. (2004). Improving Competitiveness of Indian Higher Education in the Global Market. Paper presented in National Conference on *"Internationalization of Higher Education: Issues and Concerns"* held at National Institute of Educational Planning and Administration (NIEPA), New Delhi.

Azad, J.L. (2004). Privatization of Higher Education. in Venkatasubramanian K. (ed.), *Issues in Higher Education, Vol.I*, Hyderabad: The ICFAI University Press.

Balasubramanyam, V.N. (2000). *Writings on International Economics*, Oxford University Press, New Delhi.

Becker, Rosa (2009). International Branch Campuses: Marketing and Strategies. *The observatory on Borderless Higher Education*, London:40.

Becker, Rosa (2010). International Branch Campuses: New Trends and Directions. International Higher Education, *The Boston College Centre for International Higher Education,* No.58, Winter 2010: 03-05.

Bhalla, Veena (2003). International Students in Indian Universities, 2001-02. *Higher Education Policy and Practices*, 01 (1-2): 71-72.

Bhaskar, Rao D. (2001). *Distance Education in Different Countries*, New Delhi: APH Publishing Corporation.

Bhattachary, Joyati (2012). Higher Education in India: Issues, Concerns and Remedies. *University News*, 50 (17): 01-04.

Bhushan, Subhanshu (2004). Trade in Educational Services under GATS: Implications for Higher Education in India. *Economic and Political Weekly*, 39 (21).

Bhushan, Subhanshu (2005). *Research Study Report Foreign Education Providers in India.* New Delhi: National Institute of Educational Planning and Administration.

Biswas, Chandra (2001). Internationalization of Higher Education: A Case of WTO's Sectoral Impact on Higher Education of India, in Panduranga Rao D. (ed.), *WTO and Competitiveness: Challenges for Indian Business and Management Education*, New Delhi: Excel Books: 483-489.

Bok, Derek (2003). *Universities in the Market Place: The Commercialization of Higher Education*, Princeton and Oxford: Princeton University Press.

Bolashetty S. Shripad (2005a). Trade in Indian Higher Education Service Sector: Implications of WTO's GATS, Part-I. *University News,* 43 (36): 01-08.

Bolashetty S. Shripad (2005b). Trade in Indian Higher Education Service Sector: Implications of WTO's GATS, Part-II. *University News*, 43 (38): 06-14.

Chalam, K.S. (2004). Privatization of Higher Education under WTO Regime. *University News*, 42 (07).

Chanda, Rupa (1999). Movement of Natural Persons and Trade in Services: Liberalising Temporary Movement of Labour under the GATS. *Working Paper No.51,* Indian Council for Research on International Economic Relations (ICRIER), New Delhi.

Chanda, Rupa (2004). General Agreement on Trade in Services: Implications for Social Policy-Making. *Economic and Political Weekly*, 39 (21).

Chen, Tse-mei and Barnett A. George (2000). Research on International Student flows from a Macro Perspective: A network analysis of 1985, 1989 and 1995. *Higher Education,* 39 (01).

Chindhade, S.V. (2004). Impact of Privatization on Education in India: Some Stray Thoughts. *University News*, 42 (07).

Currie, Jan and Newson Janice (1998). *Universities and Globalization: Critical Perspectives,* New Delhi: SAGE Publication.

Dachi, A.H. (2000). Students Loans in Higher Education Finance in Tanzania: A Delusion, or a Hidden Benevolent Grant Scheme?. *Perspectives in Education*, 16 (03).

Dagar, B.S. and Dhull Indira (1999). Some Reflections on World Declaration on Higher Education for the 21st Century: Vision and Action. *University News*, 03 (51).

Damme, Dirk Van (2001). Quality issues in the Internationalization of Higher Education. *Higher Education*, 41 (04).

Dasgupta, A.K. (2004). Is there a Case for For-Profit Private University?. *University News*, 42 (07).

Daun, Holger (2002). *Educational Restructuring in the Context of Globalization and National Policy,* New York and London: Routledge Falmer.

De Ville Philippe, Mortou Francois and Vandenenberghe Vincent (1996). Cost-benefit Analysis and regulatory Issues of Student Mobility in the EU. *European Journal of Education*, 31 (02).

Dharmadhikary, S. (2004). GATS and Social Policy-Making. *Economic and Political Weekly*, 39 (21).

Dhar, Santosh and Dhar Upinder (2001). WTO and Education: Emerging Trends. in Panduranga Rao D. (ed.), *WTO and Competitiveness: Challenges for Indian Business and Management Education*, New Delhi: Excel Books: 502-510.

Gaba, A.K. and Bhushan B. (2004). Funding of Open and Distance Higher Education in India: Quality and Policy Issues. *University News*, 42 (08).

Gananam, A. (2004). Privatization in Relation to Globalization in Indian Context. *University News*, 42 (07).

Goel, Aruna and Goel S.L. (2005). *Encyclopaedia of Higher Education in the 21st Century,* Vols. I and II, New Delhi: Deep and Deep Publications Pvt. Ltd.

GoI (1986). *National Policy on Education 1986.* New Delhi: Ministry of Human Resource Development, Government of India.

GoI (1998). *Indian Students/Trainees Going Abroad.* New Delhi: Department of Education, Planning, Monitoring and Statistics Division, MHRD. (Various Issues: 1986-87, 87-88, 88-89, 89-90, 90-91, 91-92, 92-93, 93-94, 94-95, 95-96, 96-97, 97-98, 98-99).

GoI (2002). *Tenth Five Year Plan 2002-07. Vol.II,* New Delhi: Planning Commission, Government of India.

GoI (2003a). *University Development in India: Basic Facts and Figures.* New Delhi: University Grants Commission, Government of India.

GoI (2003b). *Statistical Abstract.* New Delhi: University Grants Commission, Government of India.

GoI (2005). *Selected Educational Statistics 2003-04.* New Delhi: Ministry of Human Resource Development, Government of India.

GoI, *Various Reports of Five Year Plans,* New Delhi: Planning Commission.

Gopal, K. (2000). Anatomy of the Indian University Education. *Perspective in Education*, 16 (02).

Gordon, Jean and Jollade Jean-Pierre (1996). Spontaneous Student Mobility in the European Union: A Statistical Survey. *European Journal of Education*, 31 (02).

Gosai, M.R. (2004). Privately Promoted Indian Higher Education: Some Legal and Ethical Perceptions. *University News*, 42 (07).

Gupta, Asha (2004). Judicialization of Higher Education in India: A Bane or a Boon, paper presented in National Conference on *"Internationalization of Higher Education: Issues and Concerns"* held at National Institute of Educational Planning and Administration (NIEPA), New Delhi.

Gupta, K.R. (2000). *World Trade Organisation (Text)*, New Delhi: Atlantic Publishers and Distributors.

Gupta, Pradeep (2011). Status of Higher Education in India: An Appraisal. *University News*, 49 (37): 11-13.

Hang, Guy (1996). Student Mobility between Europe and the US. *European Journal of Education*, 31 (02).

Hegde, B.M. (2001). The Export of Indian Higher Education in K.B Powar (ed.), *Internationalization of Indian Higher Education*, Association of Indian Universities, New Delhi.

Henry, Mirian, Lingard Bob, Rizvi Fazal and Taylor Sandra (2001). *International Association of Universities Issues in Higher Education: The OECD, Globalisation and Education Policy,* Queensland University.

http://www.dfat.gov.au/trade/negotiations/ministerial/doha_info_paper_outcomes.html

Hussain, S. (2000). Challenges before Higher Education. *University News*, 38 (38): 14-15.

IDP (2002). *Education Australia 2002.* The Global Student Mobility 2025.

Iyer, V.R. and Gopalakrishnan P.G. (2004). Higher Education in a Liberalized Economy. *University News*, 42 (01).

Jackson, H. John (1999). Designing and Implementing Effective Dispute Settlement Procedures: WTO Dispute Settlement, Appraisal and Prospects. in Krueger O. Anne (ed.), *The WTO as an International Organization*, Calcutta: Oxford University Press.

Jarvis, Peter (2001). *Universities and Corporate Universities: The Higher Learning Industry in Global Society,* London: Stylus Publishing.

Jinah, Seol (2005). Barriers to the Internationalization of Traditional Higher Education and Opportunities for ODE. ICDE International Conferrence, New Delhi.

Kaushik, Madhulika (2004). GATS and Cross Broader Supply (Mode-I) in Higher Education: Strategies and Implications. Paper presented in National Conference on *"Internationalization of Higher Education: Issues and Concerns"* held at National Institute of Educational Planning and Administration (NIEPA), New Delhi.

Khadria, Binod (2004). Paradoxes and Pitfalls in Internationalization of Higher Education under the WTO Regime of Trade in Services: A Critical Analysis of Mode III and Mode IV. Paper presented in National Conference on *"Internationalization of Higher Education: Issues and Concerns"* held at National Institute of Educational Planning and Administration (NIEPA), New Delhi.

Khajapeer, M. (2004). GATS in Higher Education in India: Some Implications. in R.V. Dadibhavi and S.T. Bagalkoti (ed.), *WTO Implications on India,* Karnataka University, Dharwad: 42-52.

Knight, Jane (2003). *A Report of GATS, Trade and Higher Education Perspective 2003—Where are We?.* The Observatory on Borderless Higher Education, London, United Kingdom.

Knight, Jane (2002). Trade in Higher Education Services: The Implications of GATS. *The Observatory on Borderless Higher Education,* London: United Kingdom 2004.

Knight, Jane (2006). *Higher Education Crossing Borders: A Guide to the Implications of the General Agreement on Trade in Services (GATS) for Cross-border Education: A Report prepared for Commonwealth of Learning and UNESCO,* Commonwealth of Learning and UNESCO, Canada and Paris.

Kripal, V. (2005). Quality in Higher Education: A Right of the Stakeholder. *University News*, 43 (38).

Kumar, Anil (1999). Open University Distance Learners' Attitude towards Distance Education. *Perspective in Education*, 15 (03).

Kyung, Wonseon (1996). In-Migration of College Students to the State of New York. *Journal of Higher Education*, 67 (03).

Mannivannan, D.G. (2004). The Implications of GATS Trade in Higher Education Services: The Indian Perspective of Private Participation. *University News*, 42 (07).

Mathang, Seshagiri (2006). Foreign Students root for Karnataka. *The Times of India*, Karnataka, December 07.

Meena (2005). Responding to GATS. *University News*, 43 (01): 05-10.

Mehrotra, S. (2005). Human Capital or Human Development. Search for a Knowledge Paradigm for Education and Development. *Economic and Political Weekly*, 32 (19).

Mudaliar, A. Lakshmanaswami (1960). *Education in India*, Bombay: Asian Publishing House.

Mukherjee, Neela (2000). *World Trade Organization and India's Trade Policy in Services*, New Delhi: Vikas Publishing House Pvt. Ltd.

Naidov Vik (2010). Transnational Higher Education: Why it happens and who Benefits. *The Boston College Centre for International Higher Education*, No.58, Winter 2010: 06-07.

Narag, A.S. (2001). International Students at the University of Delhi. in K.B Powar (ed.), *Internationalization of Indian Higher Education*, Association of Indian Universities, New Delhi: 190-192.

Natarajan, R. (1998). Internationalization of Engineering Students. *Journal of Higher Education*, 21 (01).

Neave, Guy and Frans A. Van Vught (ed.), (1994). *Government and Higher Education Relationships across three Continents: The Winds of Changes,* IAU Press, Pergamon.

Nuna, Sheel (2004). Trade in Educational Services under GATS with Particular reference to Mode 3 Commercial Presence and Mode 4 Presence of Natural Person, paper presented in National Conference on *"Internationalization of Higher Education: Issues and Concerns"* held at National Institute of Educational Planning and Administration (NIEPA), New Delhi: 109-121.

Nyborg, Per (1996). International Student Mobility: The Nordic Experience. *European Journal of Education*, 31 (02).

Organization for Economic Co-operation and Development, (OECD Observer) Policy Brief, (August 2004), *"Internationalization of Higher Education",* www.oecd.org/bookshop.

Pai, M. Ramdas (2001). The Export of Higher Education: The Experience of the Manipal Education and Medical Group in K.B Powar (ed.), *Internationalization of Indian Higher Education*, Association of Indian Universities, New Delhi.

Pani, B.S (1998). Privatization—Some Issues. *Journal of Higher Education*, 21 (02).

Parsons, Christine and Fidler Brian (2005). A New Theory of Educational Change—Punctuated Equilibrium: The Case of the Internationalization of Higher Education Institutions. *British Journal of Educational Studies*, 53 (04).

Patel, Sujata (2004). Higher Education at the Crossroads. *Economic and Political Weekly*, 39 (21).

Pawar, K.B. (2000). The idea of University. *Perspectives in Education*, 16 (03).

Pawar, K.B. (2004). Domestic Regulations Relating to Foreign Providers of Higher Education in India, paper presented in National Conference on *"Internationalization of Higher Education: Issues and Concerns"* held at National Institute of Educational Planning and Administration (NIEPA), New Delhi: 43-52.

Pawar, Sanjay K. (2010). Marketing of Higher Education through Off-shore Campuses. *University News,* 48 (06): 10-12.

Prasad, M. V.S. (2001). Internationalization of Higher Education: The IGNOU Experience in K.B. Powar (ed.) *Internationalization of Indian Higher Education*, Association of Indian Universities, New Delhi: 490-501.

Prasad, M.S.V. (2001). Globalization of Higher Education: Role of Universities. in Panduranga Rao D. (ed.), *WTO and Competitiveness: Challenges for Indian Business and Management Education*, New Delhi: Excel Books.

Qamar, Furqan (2004), "Foreign Direct Investment in Higher Education: Issues, Implications and Strategies", paper presented in National Conference on *"Internationalization of Higher Education: Issues and Concerns"* held at National Institute of Educational Planning and Administration (NIEPA), New Delhi.

Qureshi. Zahir A., and Mushtaq Luqmani (2008). The Cycle of Business Education in Malaysia: Institutional Development and Marketing Strategies. *Journal of Management Development*, 28 (10): 897-915.

Raghavan, Hema (2011). Liberalization, Privatization and Globalization of Eaucation: An Assessment. *University News*, 49 (37): 08-10.

Rajurohit, B.S. and R. Suri (2005). Footprints in Time: Generating Intellectual Capacity by Boosting Finance for Higher Education, *University News*, Vol. 42, No. 52.

Reddy, Sudarsana G., Reddy Raghunatha S., and B.M. Ramamurty (2005), "GATS and Management Education: Opportunities and Challenges", *University News*, Vol. 43, No.19.

Robertson, L. Susan, Bonal Xavier and Dale, Roger (2002), "GATS and the Education Service Industry: The Politics of Scale and Global Reterritorialization", *Comparative Education Review,* Vol. 46, No. 4, pp. 472-496.

Sahni, Rohini and Kale, Sumita (2004). GATS and Higher Education Some Reflections. *Economic and Political Weekly*, 39 (21): 2174-2180.

Sahoo, P.K. and Patil S.S. (1996). Futures of Openness in Distance Education System: A Comparative Study of ICC and CE, Mysore and IGNOU. *Perspective in Education*, 12 (03).

Sethi, Priyanka and Saharan Surender Kumar (2010). "Development of Higher Education through Five Year Plans". *University News*, 48 (51): 08-14.

Sharma, G.D. (1998). Contribution of Higher Education in National Development. *Journal of Higher Education*, 21 (02).

Sharma, H.D. and Maheshwari, L.K. (2004). Analysis of Trends in Transnational Education and Trade in Education Services. *University News*, 42 (07): 137-142.

Sharma, Sheetal (2006). Do we have enough jobs?. *University News*, 44 (38).

Shivkumar, V. (2001). Relevance of Indian Higher Education to Foreign Students and Scholars in K.B Powar (ed.), *Internationalization of Indian Higher Education*, Association of Indian Universities, New Delhi.

Shollapur, M.R. (2010). Foreign Direct Investment in Higher Education: Innovations in Design and Quality. *University News*, 48 (46): 12-16.

Sikidar, S. and Nath G. (2004). Privatization in Higher Education: Globalization, WTO, and GATS in Indian Scenario. *University News*, 42 (07).

Sodha, Singh Mahendra (2003). Feasibility of a Self-financed and Private Professional University in Uttaranchal: A Case Study. *Higher Education Policy and Practices*, 01 (1-2).

Srinivas, G. (2000). SWOT Analysis of Indian Higher Education. *University News*, 38 (48).

Srinivas, G. (2011). Revamping Funding Pattern in Higher Education. *University News,* 49 (45): 08-09.

Srisa-An, Wichit (1995). Academic Mobility in South-East Asia and the Role of Thai Higher Education in Blumenthal P. et al. (ed.), *Academic Mobility in a Changing World: Regional and Global Trends*, London and Bristol, Pennsylvania: Jessica Kingsley Publishers.

Stamenka, Uvalic-Trumbic (2002). *Globalization and the Market in Higher Eduation: Quality, Accreditation and Qualifications*, UNESCO Publishing, Paris.

Stastna, Vera (2001). Internationalization of Higher Education in the Czech Republic—the impact of European Union Programmes. *European Journal of Education*, 36 (04).

Stella, Antony (2004). Cross-Border Education: Is it a non-Issue?. *University News*, 42 (07).

Sukhadeo, Thorat (2006). *Higher Education in India: Emerging Issues Related to Access, Inclusiveness and Quality.* Paper presented on the occasion of Nehru Memorial Lecture, University of Mumbai, November, 24, 2006, Mumbai.

Sukumar, B. (2005). Distance Education *vis-à-vis* Global Trends: Means for India, ICDE International Conference, New Delhi.

Supriya, M.V. (2001). "The General Agreement on Trade in Services and The Education Sector", in Panduranga Rao D. (ed.), *WTO and Competitiveness: Challenges for Indian Business and Management Education*, Excel Books, New Delhi.

Takwale, R. (1998). Partnership with Foreign Providers for Extending Higher Education. *Journal of Higher Education*, 21 (02): 151-163.

Teichler, Ulrich (1996). Student Mobility in the Framework of ERASMUS: findings of an evaluation study. *European Journal of Education*, 31 (02).

Thakur, Ghanshyam (2004). *Challenge and Problems in Higher Education in India*, New Delhi: Sanjay Prakashan.

Tilak, J.B.G. (1993). Financing Higher Education in India: Principles, Practice, and Policy Issues. *Higher Education*, 26.

Tilak, J.B.G. (2003). Higher Education and Development in Asia. *Journal of Educational Planning and Administration*, 17 (02).

Tilak, J.B.G. (2004). Higher Education between the State and the Market. *UNESCO Forum Colloquium on Research and Higher Education Policy*, UNESCO Publication.

Tilak, J.B.G. (2010). The Foreign Educational Institutions Bill: A Critique, *Economic and Political Weekly*, XLV (19): 12-15.

Trivedi, H. Parimal (2010). Indian Higher Education at Cross Roads. *University News*, 48 (06): 07-08.

Uliveppa, H.H. and Siddalingappanavar M.N. (2006). GATS in Asian Countries: A case of Internationalization of Higher Education in India (A SWOT Analysis) in Talwar Sabanna (ed.), *Globalization and WTO, Vol. II,* New Delhi: Serial Publications: 506-514.

UNESCO, (2001). *"Policy Paper for Change and Development in Higher Education",* UNESCO, Paris.

Usha, Devi M.D. (2011). Foreign Universities in India: Challenges before the Indian Government. *University News*, 49 (09): 14-15.

Vivek, P.S. (2003). Promoting Higher Education: Can University Preparatory Courses be An Answer? *Perspectives in Education,* 19 (03).

Welch, Anthony (2002). Going Global? Internationalizing Australian Universities in a Time of Global Crisis. *Comparative Education Review*, 46 (04).

Wende, Marijk, Van Der (1996). Mobility Reviewed: Trends and Themes in the Netherlands. *European Journal of Education*, 31 (02).

What WTO, Ministerial Meet mean to India? Tuesday, March 7 2006, http://rss.oneindia.in/http://rss.oneindia.in/

Wilson, D.N. (2003). The Future of Comparative and International Education in a Globalised World. *International Review of Education*, 47 (1-2).

World Bank (2000). *Higher Education in Developing Countries: Peril and Promise.* The Task Force on Higher Education and Society, Washington, DC.

World Trade Organization, Ministerial Conference, Information Paper, Outcomes of the Fourth WTO Ministerial Conference, Doha, Qatar, 9-14 November, December 2001, Overview.

Yi. Cao. (2011). "Branch Campuses in Asia and the Pacific: Definitions, Challenges and Strategies." *Comparative and International Higher Education*, 03 (2011).

Ziguras, Christopher (2005). International Trade in Education Services: Governing the Liberalization and Regulation of Private Enterprise in Apple W. Michael, Kenway Jane and Singh Michael (ed.), *Globalizing Education: Policies, Pedagogies and Politics*, Peter Lang Publishing, Inc., New York.

Index